THE LIFE AND TIMES OF JAMIE OLIVER

Jamie Oliver is a hard man to avoid. As a chef and passionate food campaigner, he is one of the best known faces on British television. So much so that even those who stubbornly resisted his TV output probably have a pretty good idea of what they're missing.

Thanks to a combination of programme trailers, chat show appearances, and acres of press coverage, most non-believers are aware that the young Oliver had a penchant for sliding down spiral staircases and riding his Italian scooter across an uber-trendy London in search of new food experiences. Oliver resisters probably also know that as the young man matured, he committed his own time and money to train unemployed teenagers to work in high class restaurants, and later campaigned for healthy school meals and improved animal welfare standards. Above all, fans and detractors alike know that 'our Jamie' speaks in the unschooled voice of ordinary British people. If you want to hear words such as 'pukka', 'malarkey' and 'luvvly jubbly' spoken over the preparation of 'Rosemary Skewered Monkfish', then Oliver is your man.

And the truth is that there can be very few people in the United Kingdom who haven't watched at least a few episodes of an Oliver series. Equally, there probably aren't that many households that don't have one or more of his many best-selling cookery books sitting on their shelves or kitchen worktops. For fans, they are a must-have adjunct to his TV shows. For everyone else, they represent a handy Christmas present for wife, husband, girlfriend, or beloved aunt.

Those who know his work realize that there's a lot more to the man than scooters and Essex slang. Yes, it was his youth, brash energy and man-of-the-people charm that won over hearts and minds when he first appeared on British television. But behind

THE UNAUTHORIZED GUIDE TO DOING BUSINESS THE JAMIE OLIVER WAY

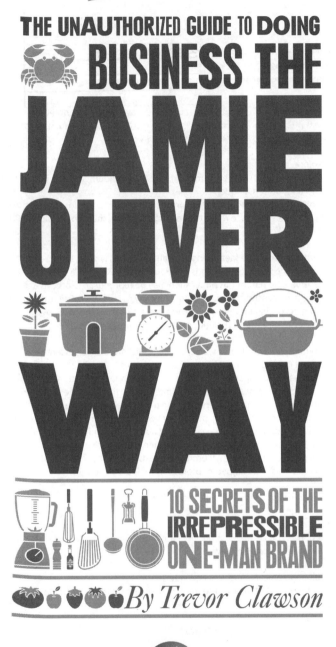

10 SECRETS OF THE IRREPRESSIBLE ONE-MAN BRAND

By Trevor Clawson

This edition first published 2010
© 2010 Trevor Clawson
First edition published 2010

The Unauthorized Guide To Doing Business the Jamie Oliver Way is an unofficial, independent publication, and Capstone Publishing Ltd is not endorsed, sponsored, affiliated with or otherwise authorized by Jamie Oliver.

Registered office
Capstone Publishing Ltd. (A Wiley Company), The Atrium, Southern Gate, Chichester, West Sussex, PO19 8SQ, United Kingdom
For details of our global editorial offices, for customer services and for information about how to apply for permission to reuse the copyright material in this book please see our website at www.wiley.com.

Library of Congress Cataloguing-in-Publication Data

Clawson, Trevor.
  The unauthorized guide to doing business the Jamie Oliver way : 10 secrets of the irrepressible one man brand / Trevor Clawson. -- 1st ed.
     p. cm.
  Includes bibliographical references and index.
  ISBN 978-1-907312-41-0 (pbk. : alk. paper) 1. Branding (Marketing) I. Title.
  HF5415.1255.C53 2010
  658.8'27--dc22
                        2010000253

A catalogue record for this book is available from the British Library.

Set in Myriad Pro by Sparks (www.sparkspublishing.com)
Printed in Great Britain by TJ International Ltd, Padstow, Cornwall

CONTENTS

the Essex wide boy persona, there was lot more going on. When the BBC's *The Naked Chef* hit our screens, he was already a skilled food professional, with experience in quality restaurants. Equally important, cooking was a passion and he clearly believed that good food should be a part of everyone's lives, regardless of age, class or income.

Over time, Oliver built on that passion and sense of mission. The early recipe shows gave way to reality TV/documentary hybrids that took our hero into deeper and darker territory. Prompted by a desire to give something back, he established a restaurant to train unemployed and (sometimes) underprivileged teenagers to work in kitchens. He persuaded cabinet ministers to invest more in school meals. He shocked an invited audience by gassing chickens live on stage to demonstrate the reality behind intensive food pro-duction. He even taught the people of Rotherham to cook.

Today, the perkiness and enthusiasm are still there. The man who cooked to a rock 'n' roll beat in *The Naked Chef* happily donned the attire of each member of US disco band the Village People to promote a series of shows. But the deeper side has transformed Oliver from fast food into a much more subtle and flavoursome dish. He still divides opinion between those who love his brash charm and those who hate it, but he has achieved the status of a national treasure.

A PERFECTLY PUKKA BUSINESSMAN

But he's something else as well. Along the way, he's also proved himself as a businessman. The proof lies on the high street. In the early days of his career, Oliver was essentially selling himself – in the form of his TV shows, DVDs and books. In selling himself he not only claimed his place on the top tier of the celebrity cake, he also established a brand that could be used to sell products and services on the back of his name and reputation. Those products have become increasingly diverse. Once we've bought the DVD and acquired the cookbook, we can also purchase his branded saucepans, barbeque equipment, mugs, sauces and oils. We can even buy an Oliver video game and download his cooking advice onto our mobile phones.

If you want to hear the words such as 'pukka', 'malarkey' and 'luvvly jubbly' spoken over the preparation of rosemary skewered monkfish, then Oliver is your man

In short, he presides over a pretty extensive and lucrative empire. Figures filed at Companies House show that in 2007, Oliver's Holding Company recorded a profit of £3.07m, a figure that doubled to £6.8m the following year. That's just part of the story. When you add up his assets he is a very wealthy young man indeed. In 2009 the *Sunday Times Rich List* estimated his fortune at £40m, despite recession and tumbling property prices.

He's also proud of the fact that he employs a lot of people across his TV Production Company, holding company, restaurants and stores. Speaking to the *Daily Telegraph* in January 2009 he said: 'I've always invested in people. Ten years ago, I had no one … by the end of this year, it will be 5500.'[1]

It's Oliver's success as a businessman that we'll be looking at in this book.

THE MAN AND THE BRAND

At the heart of Oliver's success is the creation of a hugely powerful brand based around his communication skills. He has a gift for addressing a TV audience in a natural voice without the aid of a script and by harnessing his fluidity as a presenter to a passion for the subject, he has become a trusted guide to the worlds of cooking and food production. From that simple beginning Oliver the man has evolved into Oliver the brand.

We'll be looking at how he has achieved that later in the book, but before going any further it's worth looking at why Oliver's career is instructive to just about anyone running a business or striving to get ahead within an organization.

You don't need me to tell you that we live in the age of the brand. A quarter of a century ago, it was a word that was barely used by consumers. Today it's a different story. The big corporations who sell us our clothes, our chocolate, our cars and even our motor insurance spend a huge amount of time promoting themselves as brands rather than product providers. They want us to engage with them as brands, to join their communities or social networks and to act as advocates – recommending them to friends.

And by and large we play the game. As consumers we're happy to talk about the brands we're loyal to. We even join or form brand communities on social network sites such as Facebook or Myspace.

We are what we consume and the brands we choose help to both fix our position within a tribe whilst differentiating us from others.

In other words, they help define who we are and who we are not. At the same time, they also demonstrate to the world how well we've done, how much disposable income we've got to splash around, and to some extent what our values are.

The question is, of course, what distinguishes one brand from another? In some cases it's an easy sell. We can see pretty much at once that an Aston Martin is a very distinct product when compared to a Ford Focus or a Renault Megane. In other cases, it's a lot trickier. How, for example, do you distinguish between computers made by two different companies when they share the same parts and are made in the same factory in China? Or what separates two cans of beans, made in the same Norfolk factory, using identical ingredients but bearing different labels?

At one level, branding is about product, but it is also about a range of other things. It's about the image the company presents to the world, its record on customer care, its reputation for reliability and (increasingly important) it's stance on ethical matters such as waste management and climate change, wages paid to factory workers in developing countries, and so on. These are what is known as 'brand values' and they shape our perception of a product and a company.

Personalities can play a huge part in selling a company. Why is Apple generally considered to be a cooler company that Microsoft? Well, to some extent it is down to history. Apple produced a computer with an easy to use, icon-based operating system at a time when anyone using a Microsoft/IBM-style PC had to learn dozens of text-based command lines. Even switching from one application to another was a chore. Thus Apple could offer computing for the people, while Microsoft seemed to be doing it for the geeks and technocrats.

But while Microsoft's Windows has long since caught up with Apple's operating system in terms of user friendliness, there is still a 'coolness' gap between the two companies.

That's partly because Apple loads its operating system into sleek, highly designed computers, music players and phones while Windows is the engine behind millions of faceless office machines. But it's also about the founders of these companies themselves. Bill Gates and Apple's Steve Jobs are both visionaries in their own right, but somehow it's the Apple boss who wears that mantle most appealingly. Apple computers have long been the choice of people in creative industries such as publishing, advertising, design and film making. Creative computer users prefer Apple machines because of their performance and style, but they also identify with Steve Jobs. He feels like one of them.

When we enter the world of the modern entrepreneur, corporate and personal branding often walk hand-in-hand with one another

So, people have brands too – and not just the Jamie Olivers, Jeremy Clarksons and Jordans of the world. Out in the world of work, careers depend to greater or lesser extent on how an individual is perceived by his or her colleagues, customers and trading partners. Indeed, as employment consultants increasingly tell us, success in the workplace or at the helm of a small business can depend more on how we package and present ourselves than on what we actually do.

And when we enter the world of the modern entrepreneur, corporate and personal branding often walk hand-in-hand with one another. Take the Virgin empire. It's undoubtedly a brand in its own right, but our perception of the multitude of companies that sit beneath the 'V' logo is indelibly linked to our perception of Richard Branson, the man.

Then we have the new breed of TV entrepreneurs. The popularity of shows such as *The Apprentice* and *Dragons Den* has made celebrities from people who were once known only to friends, family and trading partners. Once upon a time, Theo Paphitis was the anonymous mastermind behind the turnaround of high street brands such as Ryman and Contessa. Today he is a brand in his own right – a face that sells books, fronts magazines and draws audiences to TV shows. The same is true of fellow *Dragons Den* stars Duncan Bannatyne, James Kahn, Deborah Meadon and Peter Jones.

... he has provided us with an object lesson in how to build, maintain and refresh a personal brand while juggling the role of trusted TV presenter and businessman with products to sell

At times the personal and corporate brand are one and the same. Donald Trump famously likes to have his own surname imprinted on his major real estate projects – witness New York landmark Trump Towers; Dragon Duncan Bannatyne's flagship business is now Bannatyne's Health Clubs.

Which brings us neatly back to Jamie Oliver. Over the last ten years or so, he has provided us with an object lesson in how to build, maintain and refresh a personal brand while juggling the role of trusted TV presenter and businessman with products to sell. Indeed, Oliver has apparently effortlessly created a 'virtuous circle'. Thanks to his TV celebrity, he has launched a range of products that sell simply because their labels bear his name or image. Equally, his celebrity is enhanced by public interest in his business activities and lengthy tenure as the face of the Sainsbury supermarket chain. Enhanced celebrity means higher ratings, increased book sales and, consequently, more opportunities to expand his business empire. Later in this book we'll look at exactly how he's achieved this.

The second strand in the story is focused on the mechanics running Jamie Oliver PLC: his approach to extending the brand; his strategy for dealing with criticism and adversity; his willingness to invest in new ventures, even when Britain and the world were tipping into a deep and dark recession; the process of creating a sustainable and scalable business employing hundreds of people; the steps taken to ensure that at least parts of his empire will continue to survive and thrive, even if the founder were to retire, or fall victim to the number 10 bus that is said to lie in wait for the famous and successful. We'll be exploring in detail his approach to growing and maintaining a diverse business portfolio.

EARLY LIFE

Oliver was born in on May 25, 1975 in Clavering, Essex. His parents – Trevor and Sally Oliver – ran the village pub and restaurant, The Cricketers.

There was little remarkable about Oliver's childhood. His parents enjoyed a stable and loving relationship and worked well together as partners in the pub/restaurant business. As a child growing up in a rural village, Oliver enjoyed the freedom to explore and roam the surrounding countryside, something that would be the envy of many city kids.

By all accounts he wasn't lacking in self confidence. That was partly down to growing up in a pub rather than an isolated farmhouse or remote cottage. Even as a child, he was surrounded by customers and friends of the family. By necessity he became a people person.

But he was also something of a tearaway with a taste for practical jokes. So much so in fact that his father famously set the young Oliver to work at the age of eight in order to channel his youthful energy into constructive activity. This was by no means bad news for the boy. With a pocket full of cash he became part of the playground aristocracy at school. Oliver has mentioned in the past that his father was repulsed by the idea of giving out money and so from an early age, has learnt to earn his own money.

It wasn't long before he branched out with his own micro business. As a child of a pub landlord, he was able to buy sweets from the local wholesale cash and carry – sweets that could be resold to his secondary school peers at a profit. It was, for an eleven year old, quite an elaborate operation. He rented lockers from fellow pupils – six in all – which served as store cupboards. With a good stash of sweets stored on site he could sell his products on demand. Over time he built a business that netted him £30 a week. With another £30 coming in from The Cricketers, the eleven-year-old Oliver did pretty well for himself.

It would probably be wrong to read too much into this early venture into the world of capitalism. At one time or another, most kids come up with schemes to earn money – cleaning cars, clearing out a neighbour's garden, pitching for a paper round, etc. – and it's not necessarily an indicator of entrepreneurial spirit further down the line. That said, Oliver's operation was certainly more lucrative than most.

And Oliver was swimming in a commercially-minded sea. His father and mother were self-sufficient small business people. Their success depended on their ability to attract and retain customers by offering good food and service at affordable prices. If they failed to do that there was no one else to blame. They sank or swam on the basis of their own talents. Hard work was the order of the day.

'I left school basically not knowing anything,' Trevor Oliver told *The Guardian* in 2009. 'But because I'd worked with my father in his pub, I had the ability to earn money with my hands. Before I retire, I want to teach my grandchildren that if you want something in life, you've got to work for it.'

... as his empire has grown in size, he has surrounded himself with talented and equally hard-working people

Jamie Oliver's own school career – seriously undermined by dyslexia – was less than stellar. Famously he achieved just two GCSE passes (Art and Geology) in the crucial A to C band so when he left school at sixteen, pursuing a career that required academic qualifications was not an option.

But what he had absorbed was a strong work ethic, coupled with solid experience in the catering industry. In The Cricketers, he had started chopping vegetables in the kitchen before moving on to serving at tables and later sharing some of the cooking with the full-time chefs. At thirteen he had also found himself a job at The Starr, a pub restaurant in the Essex Village of Great Dunmow. It was there that he honed is cooking skills, even to the extent of replacing a chef who was more than ten years his senior.

So despite a lack of academic qualifications, the sixteen-year-old Oliver did have a future in the catering industry. In 1991 he began studying for a Professional Chef's Diploma at Westminster Kingsway College. It was the doorway not just to a vocational qualification but (potentially) to an exciting career with no obvious limits.

Even today, the UK catering trade has something of a mixed reputation. On the one hand, if you look across the entire spectrum of the industry – including fast food takeaways, cafes, sandwich bars – work in a kitchen or as a waiter is often equated with long hours, low status and lousy pay. But when you focus on the top tiers of the restaurant trade it's a very different story. Britain's emergence as a foodie nation – a process that began to gather pace in the boom-fuelled 1980s – has created an apparently unquenchable demand for high quality restaurants. Restaurateurs and entrepreneurs alike have rushed to meet that demand. In the seventies, finding a decent meal that didn't involve a combination of chicken and a basket was a next to impossible task, particularly if you lived outside London. Today, there are great restaurants in just about every major town and city. All of them require well-trained staff and talented chefs.

The food revolution was well underway by the time Oliver started his course at Westminster Kingsway College and if he worked hard, got his diploma then spent time honing his trade in the wider world, he could reasonably expect to make a good living.

WKC was well connected. More than 100 years old, it could offer its trainees placements at some of London's top restaurants, including old school names such as Claridges and the Savoy. The dyslexic Oliver reportedly struggled with some of the academic work required by the course – particularly the food science element – but he relished the experience across a range of kitchens and cooking styles.

THE REAL WORLD

His course completed, Oliver set out in search of a real job. His first port of call was the Neal Street Restaurant, owned by Antonio Carluccio where he worked as a pastry chef under the tutelage of Gennaro Contaldo. It was there that he learned about bread and pasta and developed an ongoing love of Italian cooking. Equally important, with the security of a wage, he could now consider moving to London rather than commuting from Essex and, in 1995, he and his girlfriend Jools moved into a small flat.

The next stage on his journey was at the River Café, a restaurant opened by Ruth Rogers and Rose Gray on the banks of the Thames. Located by the riverside in west London, this was a seriously trendy establishment, housed in a building designed by Richard Rogers. Then, as now, its focus was Italian food and the owners were committed to using the best ingredients, sourced where possible from Italy. In a radical rethink of normal design, the restaurant was built on open plan principles, with the kitchen area in full view of the dining space. In a small way, the kitchen staff could become 'stars' – or at the very least be part of the spectacle. That informality extended to the customers. They were generally a well-heeled bunch, but casual dress tended to be the order of the day.

The restaurant had a profile that extended beyond its immediate clientele. The celebrated River Café cookery books were already popular among foodies when Oliver took his job. The books helped brand the restaurant as a relaxed and hip place to wine and dine.

And it is the River Café that ultimately gave Oliver his TV break. In 1996, a BBC film crew arrived to shoot a documentary entitled *Christmas at The River Café*. Then working as a sous (under) chef, Oliver was a robust presence and he attracted the attention of the director and crew. In a series of sequences, he revealed an ability to work with the food and talk to the camera at the same time. When the documentary was broadcast in 1997, his contributions stood out. As the cameras revealed, he wasn't just a part of the furniture at the River Café, he was a star in the making.

AND THE REST IS HISTORY

Some men are born great, some achieve greatness and some have greatness thrust upon them. To that list Shakespeare could easily have added, and 'some have greatness dropped into their lap by the power of television.'

Oliver was 21 years old and his obvious ambition was still tempered by an awareness that he was learning his trade. That changed with the showing of *Christmas at The River Café*. Suddenly he was on the edge of a TV career.

The charismatic young man with Essex vowel sounds had yet to make a significant impression on the viewing public. Galling as it may be for the thousands of people who fruitlessly spend their youth, time, energy and money on auditions, interviews with agents and show reels, getting a break in television is often about luck rather than hard work. TV producers need talent. They need people who can walk, talk and address a camera simultaneously. And their problem is often identifying that talent amongst a forest of hopefuls. In Oliver's case, an appearance on a documentary had given him a show reel to die for.

And the rest is history. As a direct result of the River Café broadcast, he was signed up by production company Optomen Television. Working with producer Pat Llewellyn he recorded three series of *The Naked Chef* for the BBC. Built around his personality and a rendering of his London lifestyle, the show revitalized the TV cookery format and made Oliver a star.

It was this stardom that gave Oliver the launch pad on which to build a business empire, based on a distinct personal brand and ultimately a portfolio of business ventures.

THE DIFFERENCE ENGINE

When Oliver burst onto the TV screens he was entering a crowded universe. By the late 1990s British television was awash with celebrity chefs. From short cookery slots on breakfast and daytime TV through to peak time viewing on BBC2 and Channel 4, food was a staple in the broadcasters' diet.

Broadcasters needed chefs with the ability to impart information and enough personal style to captivate the audience, and their quest for such talent brought a diverse range of enthusiastic foodies and wine buffs onto our screens. We had school mistress types in the form of Sophie Grigson, reliable old favourites like Delia Smith. Then there were the slightly tipsy 'bon viveurs' typified by Keith Floyd and Oz Clark. The new generation of star chefs was represented by names like Ainsley Harriott, Antony Worrall Thompson, the post-punk Gary Rhodes and seafood expert Rick Stein. And coming in from left field were the Two Fat Ladies, a reminder of the way people used to lavish care on traditional British dishes.

And of course, there would be more to come. Today, Oliver shares the TV kitchen with the likes of alpha male Gordon Ramsay, old Etonian Hugh Fearnley-Whittingstall, Nigel Slater and of course domestic goddess, Nigella Lawson.

From Fanny Craddock in the 1950s and 1960s through to Graham Kerr (aka 'The Galloping Gourmet') in the 1970s, the how-to recipe show has always had a place in the TV schedules. But by the 1990s, broadcasters had stepped up a gear. For one thing, with breakfast and daytime TV firmly established, they had more airtime to fill and cookery shows and slots were a cheap and cheerful way to keep the audience entertained. More importantly, food was starting to play a more central part in British life.

That was partly down to the social and political changes wrought by the Thatcher years. The 1980s began in deep recession but as the economy recovered a new Britain began to emerge. As exemplified by the stereotype of the yuppie (the young urban professional), the UK began to develop its own downsized version of the American dream. Deregulation, and the privatization of key industries helped create a culture in which an increasing number of people – not just the captains of industry – began to think about their lives in terms of wealth creation, ambition and individualism. More people began to reject the idea of salaried jobs working for corporates and chose instead to start small businesses. The media sector expanded, creating thousands of new jobs in a trendy industry. The icon of the age was the Filofax. If you owned one of these leather-bound, loose-leaf diaries and organizers – and managed to fill it with the details of business contacts – it showed you were one of the new breed of aspirational Britons.

Like the hippies of the 1960s, the young urban professionals of the 1980s were relatively few in number when compared to those who held down less than glamorous jobs in offices or factories. But with the help of magazines and the TV, their lifestyle helped create an appetite for the good things in life – well designed furniture, cars and, of course, well-cooked and attractively presented food.

Eating out became part of the culture – something you did once or several times a week rather than once or twice a year – as did the dinner party. Suddenly it was important to know about food and wine. Lifestyle and cookery shows on British TV had a hungry audience.

THE X-FACTOR

One of the questions we'll be asking in this book is how Jamie Oliver managed to rise to the top of the cookery cauldron and stay there over the years. Equally, why is he so much richer than his peers? When recession began to bite, restaurateur and undoubted TV star Gordon Ramsay dropped out of the *Sunday Times Rich List*, leaving Oliver as the only chef on the chart.

So what has made Oliver stand out? Why has he seemingly got the 'X-factor'?

Well in terms of 'Oliver the brand', the short answer could well be that he is simply more interesting than most of his peers. That wasn't always apparent. When *The Naked Chef* was first broadcast, his appeal seemed pretty one dimensional. He was young, pretty, and energetic – and he knew his onions. The Essex banter that turned at least some potential viewers right off, was a breath of fresh air to others, and he made cooking fun.

But when you begin to look at the totality of his TV career, it becomes apparent that he has effortlessly invaded the territory of most of his TV rivals while remaining true to his own personality. Like Nigella he offers easy recipes alongside a lifestyle to die for, surrounding himself with family and friends, and inviting us in to join the party. Like Keith Floyd, he has the ability to mix travelogue with cookery – witness his recent American tour. And, in common with Gordon Ramsay, he is a master of the reality TV format with shows such as *Jamie's Kitchen* and *Jamie's School Dinners*.

... he has effortlessly invaded the territory of most of his TV rivals while remaining true to his own personality

Interest in food quality (or the lack of it) also became part of the broadcasters' remit in the 1990s, through issue-based programmes such as *Food File*. Oliver's own obsession with food quality led him to undertake a campaign to improve Britain's eating habits and attitudes to animal welfare. Today he is a figurehead for those who believe that eating good, healthy food matters to individuals, families and society as a whole. He has the ears of TV viewers and politicians alike.

So is he Saint Jamie? Well not in the sense that he sits in a hermitage believing good works alone will change society. As a businessman, he is ambitious, hard working and prepared to take risks to get what he wants. Equally importantly, as his empire has grown in size, he has surrounded himself with talented and equally hardworking people. Perhaps most importantly, Oliver has an instinctive ability to identify the course of action that is right for him and his career at any one time, and the business acumen to pursue that action to a successful conclusion.

AT A GLANCE

EARLY LIFE

- Oliver was born in May 1975, in Clavering, Essex. His parents, Sally and Trevor Oliver, ran a pub/restaurant called The Cricketers.
- At the age of eight he worked in the pub's kitchens, and graduated from chopping vegetables to serving table and, ultimately, cooking.
- At the age of 13 he got a job in The Starr, Great Dunmow.
- After leaving school at 16, he applied for and won a place at Westminster Kingsway Catering College.
- His first job was in the kitchens of the Neal Street Restaurant, working as pastry chef for Antonio Carluccio.
- He then joined the River Café in West London where he worked as a sous chef.

HIS TV CAREER

- In 1997 he appeared in a TV documentary – *Christmas at the River Café*. As a result of this appearance he was approached by TV production company, Optemon Television.
- Together with Optemon he made three series of *The Naked Chef* for the BBC, 1998–2000.
- In 2000 he signed up as the face of Sainsbury in a series of ad campaigns for the supermarket. The scheduling of the ads and the stylistic similarities to *The Naked Chef* series led to a split from the BBC.
- Live shows were taken on the road. In the period between not being recommissioned by the BBC and Channel 4 commissioning *Jamie's Kitchen*, Oliver staged a series of live shows.

- Oliver developed an idea to set up a social enterprise aimed at training teenagers. The venture centred on a restaurant called Fifteen that would employ and train disadvantaged youngsters and give them their first break. His efforts were documented on *Jamie's Kitchen* (2002, a series made by Channel 4 TV and Oliver's own Fresh One Production Company).
- *Jamie's Kitchen* was followed up with *Jamie's School Dinners* (2005), a series following Oliver's attempts to improve the quality of school meals. As a result of the campaign, the government pledged £280m extra to revitalize school canteens.
- 2008 – in *Jamie's Ministry of Food*, he travelled to Rotherham where he worked to encourage better cooking on a housing estate.
- 2008 – in *Fowl Dinners*, he used shock tactics to make consumers think about animal welfare standards.
- *Jamie's Italian Tour* (2007) and *Jamie's American Tour* (2009) explored the culinary heritage of those countries. *Jamie at Home* (2007), saw him return to the domestic recipe show format of *The Naked Chef.*

BUSINESS INTERESTS

- Jamie Oliver is now a consultant at Monte's Dining Club.
- He is also a board member and backer of the Fifteen Foundation.
- In recent years he has launched a series of business ventures, including the Recipease shop chain, Jamie's Italian and Jamie's Kitchen Restaurant chains, a party planning business, and an 'own brand' line of herbs, sauces, oils and

kitchenware. Through a partnership with Tranic Franchising, Jamie's Italian is to be rolled out across Asia.

- He has signed a number of deals with manufacturers to produce products bearing his name. These include kitchenware (with Tefal), ceramics (Royal Worcester), the Flavour Shaker (DKB Household) and barbeque equipment (Merison).
- Multimedia activities include a video game for the Nintendo DS, and video downloads for mobile phone users.

1

BE YOURSELF, BUT MORE SO

Jamie Oliver is a TV presenter with a big and likeable personality, but he is a lot more than that. Building on the success of his television shows he has established himself as powerful and bankable brand.

You won't have to venture very far out into the world before you encounter 'Oliver the brand'. Pop into the newsagent and you'll find him sitting prominently among the food and lifestyle titles, smiling from the cover of his own magazine. Take a short walk to the supermarket or local deli and you'll see his face or his personal messages adorning the labels of pasta sauce and packs of fresh herbs. Duck into the hardware shop and you could well find yourself tempted by the Tefal range of Oliver-inspired kitchenware. And depending on where you live you might end your day with a meal in one of his restaurants. Of course, you might stay at home and watch TV. The chances are you'll see him endorsing Sainsbury's supermarket in an advert or fronting one of his shows.

So where does 'Oliver the man' end and 'Oliver the brand' begin? That's actually quite a tough question. Oliver's business success is based on his own personality. His persona shone forth when he first appeared on TV in *The Naked Chef*. Love him or hate him, you couldn't ignore him – he was a TV natural.

But the character of *The Naked Chef* was giving us something more than one man's big personality. The show was first aired on BBC2, a channel that took lifestyle very seriously at the end of the 1990s. From home makeover shows and gardening through to recipe series fronted by personalities, the channel reflected Britain's growing obsession with the domestic challenge of living stylishly and well.

And *The Naked Chef* was certainly about the lifestyle. Oliver fronted the show from a trendy London flat that appeared to be populated by relatives and easy-on-the-eye friends. Later, when he moved to Channel 4, Oliver would repeat this 'fly-on-the-wall' style trick with *Jamie at Home*. This time his retreat was a bucolic idyll in the English countryside, replete with vegetable garden, chickens and its own pizza ovens.

Oliver's business success is based on his own personality

Meanwhile, projects such as *Jamie's Kitchen*, *Jamie's School Dinners* and *Jamie's Ministry of Food* have cemented Oliver's position as a campaigner for higher food standards. He is seen as someone who is cool, authentic, honest and committed. It's a persona that the public buy into not only via his television work but also through the products that bear his name.

Oliver's successful exploitation of his own brand echoes that of Britain's best known entrepreneur, Richard Branson. Like Oliver, Branson enjoys something of a personality cult. From his buccaneering challenge to British Airways' long haul business to his much publicized round-the-world ballooning efforts, he has fixed himself in the public imagination as a 'can do' adventurer who is always ready to take on industry's big hitters and offer better value to the public in the process. Like Oliver, he is unstuffy and is good at communicating with his market. Generally speaking he is well-liked and trusted, and the businesses he runs always seem to be just a bit 'cooler' than the competition.

But there are major differences. When Branson began his business career, he was marketing a student newspaper and later selling cut price records by mail order under the Virgin brand. The teenagers who lapped up the discounts on the records neither knew nor cared who Branson was. They did know the name Virgin, though. Today – even though Branson is a household name – his company's brand is still Virgin. Yes, Branson's personality enhances his appeal and his approach to business is inextricably associated with the appeal of the white V on a red background, but if the founder were to fall under a bus tomorrow the brand and all the values associated with it would survive, at least for a time.

Oliver proved himself a TV natural, not least because he could mix ingredients and talk simultaneously

In contrast Oliver is a personal brand. The TV shows, the cookbooks, the DVDs, the kitchenware and the herbs sell under his own name. If he fell victim to the same bus, a significant part of his business would lose the motor that drives its sales. And for that reason, Oliver must continue to develop and refresh that brand while keeping himself in the public eye.

CREATE AN IMAGE

The first step for Jamie Oliver was the creation of his TV persona. It has to be stressed that Oliver's personality was not manufactured for the audience. Biographers agree that he was a 'mouthy', cheeky child who grew up to be a not dissimilar adult. Thanks in part to his upbringing in an Essex pub, he had confidence and social skills in abundance. That confidence wasn't shaken by a poor academic performance in school. After all, his love of food had given him a career path that was in no way dependent on academic qualifications. He knew he could do well by working hard and working in an industry that he loved.

Realistically, he could have hoped to work his way up through the kitchens and make a decent living as a head chef, perhaps even starting his own restaurant someday. Happily for Oliver – and all of those who now rely on his activities for gainful employment – he found himself working in the kitchens of London's River Café Restaurant at a time when a TV crew were making a documentary.

Although unschooled in the dark arts of broadcasting, Oliver proved himself a TV natural, not least because he could mix ingredients and talk simultaneously. More important perhaps, he retained his personality in front of the camera. As Oliver recalled on his website, his contribution to the show drew an instant response. 'The day after the programme was shown, I got calls from five production companies all wanting to talk about a possible show. I couldn't believe it and thought it was my mates winding me up!'[1]

One of those who made contact was Pat Llewellyn, a producer at Optomen Television. Oliver was asked to test for his own series. This was when the Oliver personal brand was born.

The trick that Oliver pulls off so effortlessly is that his appearances on TV seem totally natural and as uncontrived as his recipes. You take a set – in the case of The Naked Chef, Oliver's own flat – add a tousle-headed mouthy presenter, allow him to address the camera for half an hour and hey presto, you have a 'pukka' TV show! It looked as easy as mixing these basic ingredients. Oliver wanted to show that it was possible to make good meals without having to splash out on expensive ingredients or gadgets.In fact a lot of time, effort and skill went into ensuring that the ingredients worked. Famously, the pilot show by Optemon TV for the BBC was a failure. Oliver spoke directly to camera in affected tones. It seemed stilted and unnatural.

From that low point, the winning format was developed. Oliver was determined to be himself, preparing and serving dishes for friends and relations. As he put together the recipe he entered into a dialogue with the producer off-camera. The show was buzzing with life and energy. As Oliver described it, most of the cooking was done in real time and rather than reading from an autocue, Oliver delivered his recipes unscripted and in his own style, and distinctive accent and vocabulary.

Oliver was being true to himself – starring in a non-elitist food programme aimed as much at Dagenham as it was at Hampstead or the Cotswolds. But there was plenty of TV artifice at work too. A rapidly moving camera followed Oliver as he worked, giving the series a sense of energy and a stylistic look pioneered by 'youth' TV in the 1980s.

The flat in which the series was shot was Oliver's own, but it had been acquired shortly before the series commenced, as his previous residence was considered too small and cramped to host a series that served up the London good life alongside food.[2]

His new flat was ideal, but there was one problem. The Jamie Oliver of *The Naked Chef* lived in a bachelor pad. The Jamie Oliver who inhabited the real world shared his flat with long-term girlfriend Jools. For the time being at least his partner had to pretend to be living elsewhere. It was reminiscent of the careful image making that goes on around pop stars: relationships are permitted but only if they enhance and reinforce the public image.

One of the signature features of *The Naked Chef* was the spiral staircase that linked Oliver to the world outside it. Epitomizing youth and energy, he would slide down the stairs, jump on his scooter and investigate the world outside. To the casual viewer it looked as if his neighbourhood was awash with trendy delis, fresh markets and purveyors of high quality products. In fact, the production company searched far and wide across London for food stores that would fit the image of the show. There was no attempt at fakery, and the only thing that wasn't quite as it seemed was that the shops were not all local. From a scattered community of suppliers, the producers were creating a 'foodie' London of the imagination. A place much trendier and better served than the real city.

Perhaps this is what really marks the border between 'Oliver the man' and 'Oliver the television personality'. In *The Naked Chef* he succeeded in being himself, thanks to the camera work and Oliver's own ebullient personality. The series had an edge and energy that was largely absent elsewhere in the TV cookery universe. But like just about everything on TV, what we were really looking at was 'hyper reality'.

TICKING THE BOXES

By this stage Oliver was well on the way to creating an extremely bankable personal brand. So what does that actually mean?

All of us – in one way or another – have what consultants would call a 'personal brand'. At its simplest, it is how we are perceived, whether in the workplace or in the wider world. In a professional context that perception can affect our promotion chances or the type of work that lands on our desk.

A key word here is *perception*. Some people are very good at branding themselves. They aspire to playing a certain role within an organization and set about demonstrating to all those around them that they are more than capable of fulfilling it. In other words, they package themselves for the role they intend to play.

Personal branding is equally important when you're seeking to win business – either as a customer-facing agent for an organization or a self-employed person on the hunt for customers. Potential customers will look not only at the product or service on offer, but also at the seller. Is he or she honest? Capable? A suitable long-term business partner? Likely to provide the best deal? Reliable? All these factors can make or break a sale.

And while the high-profile life of Jamie Oliver may appear to be a million miles removed from the day-to-day realities of those who don't happen to be celebrities, his success in building a marketable personal brand has lessons for just about everyone who has to make a living.

THE REAL DEAL

The key component in personal brand building is *authenticity*. Love him, like him or loathe him, Oliver has been determinedly his own man from day one of his TV career. The Essex slang and accent may seem overcooked at times but his personality on camera is more than a recognizable match with his off-screen presence.

Take this encounter, described by Simon Hattenstone in a profile of Oliver for *The Guardian* newspaper. During a photo shoot outside his restaurant, the chef is passed by a postman on his rounds. On seeing Oliver, the postman is reminded that he needs to buy some food and says so. When Oliver offers to feed him, the postman comments that he shouldn't because he's putting on weight, to which Oliver replies, 'Well, deliver that post a bit quicker and you'll lose some.'[3]

It's an unscripted exchange that could easily have taken place on one of Oliver's TV shows. It's a demonstration of how his screen persona is a natural extension of his real self. That's how he works his magic. Had the production company stuck with the format of the stilted pilot episode of *The Naked Chef*, the chances are the world would not have fallen for the charms of the real Jamie Oliver.

The same rules apply to establishing any personal brand. First and foremost, adopt a style that sits naturally on your shoulders. If you're naturally extrovert – the life and soul of any party – that's your foundation. If you're quiet but authoritative, play to that particular strength. Adopt a persona that isn't you and the chances are it won't be long before the rest of the world sees through it.

> **... his screen persona is a natural extension of his real self**

Hand in hand with authenticity is *consistency*. Over the years Oliver has evolved his brand by branching out from cookery programmes to create compelling shows about animal welfare or training unemployed teenagers to work in the county's best restaurants. But throughout that evolution, Oliver has remained a remarkably consistent character. As a public figure, he's talked about the pub-owning parents who inspired him, the chefs who mentored him and the love of food that has helped transform him from school failure to multi-millionaire. In other words, we pretty much know who he is and what drives him.

Again, the rules of personal branding apply far beyond the TV studio. Once people know who you are and what you stand for, you tamper with that perception at your peril.

MAKE YOURSELF VISIBLE

In the first instance, Oliver got lucky. In a parallel universe, if he hadn't been in the right place at the right time when a camera crew arrived at the River Café Restaurant, he could well be working anonymously in a restaurant kitchen somewhere. Doubtless he'd be doing good work and may even own the restaurant, but the Oliver brand as we know it wouldn't exist.

Part of his success has been down to his willingness to court publicity and put a significant portion of his private life into the public arena. His openness in talking about his family background has helped shape our opinion of him as an honest, hard working, ambitious and driven young man who has pulled himself up through energy and an applied love of food. His decision to include relatives, friends and partner Jools in his first TV series cemented our perception of a man whose love of food sat hand in hand with a commitment to family.

Later, depictions of family life showed more strains. In both *Jamie's Kitchen* – a series following Oliver's attempts to mould a group of unemployed teenagers into chefs – Jools reacted angrily to her husband's dedication to work at the expense of his family. Then in the celebrated *Jamie's School Dinners* series Jools was filmed crying on screen following national newspaper allegations that Oliver was having an affair with a waitress, which he publicly denied.

By that stage Oliver owned the production company that made his programmes. He has
maintained that the editorial decisions
were in the hands of his producers. That
said, you can only assume that any serious objections on his part would have
resulted in the scenes being cut.

> **Oliver knows how to get a headline while instinctively staying on the right side of the cheeky/charming versus objectionable divide**

Times have changed though. In September 2009, he told the *Mail on Sunday*,
'Jools has said "I'm not doing any more telly,
because every time I'm on, I cry or b****** you."
We're just a normal couple'.[4]

These days his life is probably less of a public drama, but Oliver
knows how to get a headline while instinctively staying on the
right side of the cheeky/charming versus objectionable divide. It's
a talent that has helped keep him in the public eye.

As such, his business career has been built on the marketing/pub-
lic relations principles that a major corporation would recognize.
You create your brand, ensure it is consistent and get out into the
public arena by the most effective means possible. It's a principle
that applies equally well to anyone in a working situation. If you're
doing a good job, exhibit a particular strength or have a good story
to tell, then show the world.

ADDING THE BEEF

Which is not to say that creating a personal brand is entirely a matter of identifying positive aspects of your personality, arranging

them on a plate and serving to a grateful audience. As any management consultant will tell you, a successful brand requires style but needs substance.

Behind the Essex vowel sounds, the Oliver brand delivered plenty in the way of substance from day one. Firstly, he clearly knew his stuff when it came to food. He had, after all, trained at some of London's best known restaurants with a view to ultimately becoming a head chef. Purists often blanched at Oliver's apparently casual way of mixing ingredients, but he was a trained professional who knew exactly what he was doing.

As his career developed, so did Oliver the man: 'I was uncomfortable with the success the public had given me. I felt obliged to give something back,' he told the *Mail on Sunday*.[5]

That 'something' was the Fifteen Restaurant – set up to train unemployed and disadvantaged teenagers – and the TV series that charted its progress. From that point on, Oliver took on a more serious mantle, that of a much deeper man with definite ideas that extended beyond food. Here was someone who was also concerned about fairness and society.

NETWORK NEWS

Oliver has also proved adept at pressing-the-flesh. Thanks to the international success of *The Naked Chef* he quickly had an address book full of celebrity acquaintances, including the (then) 'royal' film star couple, Brad Pitt and Jennifer Anniston. As time went by the speed dial on his phone extended to include the great and good of the political world. Following the *Jamie's School Dinners* series he spent time with Tony Blair, various members of the Cabinet and the then shadow Prime Minister, Michael Howard. On the international stage, he was hired by Prime Minister Gordon Brown to cook for the G20 leaders when they met in London to discuss ways and means to avert a banking crisis and steer the world out of recession.

The celebrity connections had a mixed impact on Brand Oliver. During his darkest hours – the period during which the BBC did not recommission *The Naked Chef* and Channel 4 picking up on *Jamie's Kitchen* – critics with an axe to grind would often compare and contrast the 'man of the people' persona projected by Oliver with the reality of his newly gilded, jet set life.

Those critics were largely silenced by the emergence of a second-generation, campaigning Oliver. By then, he was demonstrating his ability to change things and achieve good in the world, so few people lost sleep at the thought of him schmoozing with Brad and Jennifer or chewing the fat with Tom Cruise. Meanwhile the heavyweight contacts simply enhanced his new heavyweight image. Here was a man who could meet and discuss serious issues with prime ministers and business leaders.

Equally important, his contact list gave him the clout he needed to achieve his goals.

MAKING A PACKET

These days, Oliver is about much more than TV shows and tie-in books and DVDs. He has numerous successful businesses that sell real products in the rough, tough commercial world of the high street.

The jump from celebrity and author to the face on the label of a product isn't necessarily an easy one to make. As a TV personality, Oliver established himself as authentic and passionate about food (and just about everything associated with it). He was also trusted by a public who valued his insistence on using the best possible ingredients, responsibly sourced. As such, he was (and is) an ideal figurehead for a range of businesses from restaurants to cooking sauces.

But the question that anyone in Oliver's position has to ask is 'how best do I take the brand values that I've established as a TV presenter and apply them to products on sale on a supermarket shelf?'

The answer, in the case of his supermarket range of herbs and sauces, has been to retain the apparent intimacy and informality of his relationship with the TV audience. Working with brand consultancy The Plant, Oliver has developed a set of brand guidelines for the products he creates, designs and/or endorses. He even has his own 'brand bible'. In the case of 'Jamie Oliver foods', the guidelines manifest themselves as 'personal messages from Jamie' rather than conventional labels. As on TV, Oliver is talking to you, not at you.

... he has succeeded in taking his original brand values – essentially those of the presenter and showman – and harnessed them to commercial marketing campaigns

A personal message from the founder is by no means a new concept. Who can forget the cheesy splendour of the late Victor

Kiam, owner of Remington, declaring 'I liked the shaver so much I bought the company' on ad slots? Today that type of ad is probably too redolent of US-style hard sell to impress many British consumers, but there have been plenty of more subtle variations on the theme.

Witness the appeal of Boden clothes. The mail order company sells a fine range of clothing which appeals to that portion of middle England that hankers after casual English style with a contemporary designer edge. Sales of the company's products have been helped immensely by founder Johnny Boden's commentary on the products as they appear in the company's catalogues. Here is the old Etonian founder presenting his vision directly to customers and it works a treat.

Witness, too, the clever branding of Innocent drinks. Here is a company founded on the belief that UK consumers would flock to buy fruit smoothies that were both delicious and nutritious. The selling point is natural product. Whether selling juices, smoothies, ice cream and (latterly) ready meals the company prides itself on the absence of artificial ingredients. The company also embraces ethical trading. Again, the use of apparently personal messages on the packaging, which speak directly to the consumer, are an important component in the marketing mix and enhance the company's profile as one run by enthusiastic young people, rather than a faceless conglomerate.

This kind of marketing suits Oliver's personal brand down to the ground and in addition to label design, his communication skills are harnessed through video messages and editorial both on his websites and those of the companies he partners with.

In doing so, he has succeeded in taking his original brand values – essentially those of the presenter and showman – and harnessed them to commercial marketing campaigns.

THE BRAND'S THE THING

Brought up in the 'can do' eighties and nineties, Jamie Oliver is confident, brash and possessed of a tongue that can be sharp, witty and raw in equal measure. Those are attributes he shares with millions of other working and lower middle class kids but unlike the overwhelming majority, he's created a marketable, bankable brand that he uses to sell himself and a range of products. This is how he did it:

- **Get a lucky break**. Oliver was undoubtedly lucky. But for an appearance on a TV documentary – *Christmas at The River Café* – he would well have languished in relatively prosperous obscurity had he made his way through the hierarchy of restaurant life.
- **Get the formula right.** Once discovered by a TV production company, Oliver worked with his new mentors to create a television series with a style that would complement and bring out the best from his own personality.
- **Play to your strengths.** Oliver used his lifestyle – that of a young ambitious Londoner – and created a heightened version of it for a programme. It wasn't all about scooters and spiral staircases. By cooking for family and friends, he hammered home his message that meals were an important social experience. These elements attracted a broad constituency of viewers from middle England to inner-city urban.

- **Be consistent.** Oliver's personality and brand have changed over time but it has been evolution rather than revolution. The passions that drive him today – love of food and a belief that the good life is to be enjoyed by everyone – were apparent in his early interviews and TV programmes.
- **Give substance to the brand.** Oliver was a trained chef and despite his casual approach to cooking his culinary knowledge was clearly extensive.
- **Stay visible.** By staying in the public eye Oliver broadened his appeal.
- **Leverage your brand values.** Once his career as a TV presenter was established, Oliver branched out into food products, kitchenware and a range of other ventures. While the commercial ventures are separate from his TV work, he has successfully applied the same brand values to both.

2

EXTEND THE BRAND

At the tender age of 32, Jamie Oliver made it onto the *Sunday Times Rich List* for the first time, joining chef and restaurateur, Gordon Ramsay. It was a debut that marked the young man's evolution from successful celebrity chef to formidable entrepreneur, with a string of businesses. The journalists and researchers who compiled the chart estimated that Oliver was worth something in the region of £40m.

So how exactly does a TV chef amass such a fortune? Well the short answer is that most of those who rely on television alone for their income are unlikely to find themselves among the ranks of Britain's 2000 wealthiest individuals. In the US, the stars of top rated series can command millions of dollars per episode, but in the UK the sums that change hands are much more modest. When *The Naked Chef* was first broadcast Jamie was reputedly earning just £2000 per show.

But let's not cry too many tears for television's great and good. The box in the corner provides a direct route into the hearts and minds of the viewing public. And for those who are successful and popular, regular TV appearances fuel a much larger moneymaking machine. Put a chef, gardener or motoring journalist in front of a camera and the next step is – almost inevitably – a spin-off book and DVD of the series. Add to that the revenues from chat shows and personal appearances at live events and the total return from a broadcast career begins to look a lot more appealing.

A glance at the best-seller lists reveal the power of TV to create best-selling authors, particularly in 'information genres' such as gardening and cookery. Television is, after all, a real-time medium – lose concentration and you miss that all-important ingredient or the details on where to buy that particularly attractive plant. So viewers flock to buy the book of the series where all the information is safely stored, attractively packaged and easy to access.

Of course, you can probably access the information via the web but cookery and gardening programmes are not just about useful facts, they are also in the business of selling a lifestyle. And it's a lifestyle that viewers can buy into for the £20 or so that it costs to acquire a coffee table book. OK, so you may not have a trendy pad like Jamie nor friends that look anywhere as cool, but you can leaf through *The Naked Chef* and soak up a piece of the lifestyle through words and pictures.

Jamie Oliver is more than a celebrity chef with a bankable image – he is at heart an entrepreneur

It's hardly surprising then, that the first series of *The Naked Chef* was accompanied by a book of the series, comprised of recipes that Oliver had apparently been collecting for a number of years previously. But it wasn't just about the recipes. There were glossy pictures of the chef at work and play and introductory paragraphs that conveyed the same uncut charm, enthusiasm for food and love of life and friendship that was apparent on TV.

Cashing in on a popular show doesn't necessarily require a huge amount of business acumen. Very often the spin-off book (and certainly the DVD) will be part of the business plan when the TV production company prepares its budget. All the star really has to do is negotiate a royalty, sign on the dotted line, provide whatever work is necessary and sit back as the royalties from sales flood in. In other words, the lucrative process of exploiting the personal brand of a TV star is often directed by the production company, agent or publisher rather than the celebrity at the heart of the process. That was certainly true when Oliver signed up for *The Naked Chef*.

But Jamie Oliver is more than a celebrity chef with a bankable image – he is at heart an entrepreneur. In the decade or so since his first appearance he has displayed determination to maintain as much control as possible over his business affairs while at the same time extending the potential of his main company (Jamie Oliver Holdings) to increase its revenues and profits through a string of enterprises.

In addition to the core activities of TV production and book publishing, Jamie has pressed ahead with opening restaurant chains and quality food shops, while taking time out to design a range of kitchenware products. All grist to the mill for a TV presenter who is also a trained chef and enthusiastic foodie. But his business empire has expanded into rather more surprising areas. Recently Oliver has given his name to a video game on a cookery theme and launched a series of videos downloadable to mobile phones.

In short he has used his celebrity – his personal brand – as a means to kick-start an array of different but interrelated ventures. The parallel launch of book and series was the first part of that process.

TAKE CONTROL

Oliver revealed a taste for business early in life. Inspired by his father and mother he was enterprising enough to buy sweets at wholesale prices from the cash and carry used by his parents, which he then resold in school. When he left full-time education at sixteen, that entrepreneurial spirit went on the back burner for a number of years whilst he learnt his trade as a chef.

Once the nation had taken him to its collective heart via the first *Naked Chef* TV series it quickly became apparent that he was keen to be in the commercial driving seat. The book that was tied in with series one was an immediate best-seller but Oliver seemed dissatisfied with the deal on royalties. In truth it was a fairly standard agreement. As a spin-off from a TV series, the royalties were divided between the writer and the producers. It was an arrangement that reflected that any success enjoyed by the book was due in no small part to the series itself and the investment made by the producers. As his biographers have recorded, Oliver didn't see it that way. When the time came to negotiate on the second book, Oliver had hired an agent to get a better deal regardless. By the time the third *Naked Chef* series hit the shelves, production company Optemon were no longer part of the royalties deal.[1]

He has used his celebrity – his personal brand – as a means to kick-start an array of different but interrelated ventures

On one level, Oliver's willingness to drive a hard bargain reflects nothing more than an awareness of his own rising stardom. Put simply, his celebrity was such that he could dictate terms rather than comply with the production company's standard book deal. But it was also an early indicator that as his career developed he would be very much his own man, negotiating with business partners on his own behalf and in his own best interests.

SEIZE THE MEANS OF PRODUCTION

And it wasn't long before he was taking control of the means of production too. Until 2001 his television career was dependent on third parties – notably Optemon (the production company) and the BBC. All that changed when the corporation – concerned by the chef's commercial relationship with supermarket chain Sainsbury's – declined to commission a fourth series of *The Naked Chef*. A period in the television wilderness followed and by the time Oliver made a return to the small screen in

This was cooking for the rest of us. Simple recipes that could be flung together quickly and stylishly

Jamie's Kitchen on Channel 4, his screen image was in the hands of Fresh One, his very own production company.

A joint venture between Freemantle Media and Oliver himself, Fresh One has established itself as more than a vehicle for a celebrity chef. It's certainly true that the bulk of the company's televised output has featured Oliver, but it has also expanded its brief to embrace unrelated stars and projects. For instance, sitcom actor Neil Morrissey's attempts to found and run a micro brewery were captured by the production company and aired as *Neil's Risky Business*, whilst *To the Manor Bowen* charted the progress of designer and socialite Laurence Llewelyn-Bowen as he moved his family from Greenwich to a rural idyll.

To underline the fact that Fresh One was a production company in its own right – rather than a platform for Oliver alone – the company recruited veteran producer Roy Ackerman in 2009. Speaking to *Broadcast* magazine in 2009, Ackerman admitted that establishing Fresh One as an entity that was to some extent independent of the Oliver brand would be challenging. 'The big measure of success for Fresh will be when the value of the company is not based entirely or even mainly on the stuff Jamie presents', said Ackerman.[2]

The widening of Fresh One's remit to non-Jamie related projects was undoubtedly a smart move. Regardless of how popular an individual happens to be at any given time, the tide of celebrity inevitably recedes over time – and sometimes with ruthless speed. Thus, a venture built entirely on one person's rising star has a finite shelf life. By looking beyond 'the Oliver effect' the company is securing its future as an independent producer while simultaneously increasing its potential to make profits across a range of genres.

STICK TO YOUR KNITTING

It is easy to forget that the early days of the Oliver phenomenon were not a product of the restaurant business. His breakthrough series was based around the home and cooking for friends; unlike colleagues and rivals such as Gordon Ramsay, Antony Worrall Thompson and Rick Stein, he was not a professional restaurant owner. He had been a senior employee but he had no experience of sitting in the driving seat. He certainly wasn't the head chef or restaurant owner of legend – ruling a kitchen with a terrifying rod of iron. But that was part of the appeal. This was cooking for the rest of us. Simple recipes that could be flung together quickly and stylishly.

But Oliver's extension of his personal brand into the restaurant industry was – to put it mildy – a 'no brainer'. He was, after all, a product of the restaurant industry. Arguably he began his training – albeit informally – at his parent's pub and from there he went on to work in the kitchens of another well-thought-of Essex pub/restaurant, The Starr.

Once his GCSEs were out the way, he wasted no time in enrolling for a course at Westminster Kingsway College, a gateway to further training at the Neal Street Restaurant and the River Café.

With that background, you could have expected Oliver to rush headlong into restaurant ownership, but in fact his first experience of being in the driving seat was in the role of consultant at Monte's, a private members club located on London's Sloane Street, the playground of London's moneyed establishment.

Arguably it was an unusual choice for a chef who had done more than just about anyone else to free cooking from stuffy pretension. Even the *Daily Telegraph* – a newspaper that itself wears fustiness as a badge of honour – expressed surprise. ' That the über-lad who has done much to blow away the pomposity surrounding great food should take the job of cook at a private members' club is self-evidently absurd', said journalist Matthew Norman shortly after Oliver took up his tenure in 2002. [3]

But if nothing else, Monte's allowed Oliver to sample life as the head honcho of a high profile restaurant for the first time. It was a chance to prove that he could not only talk about cooking on TV but also deliver high quality dishes to a room full of demanding diners, night after night after night. And despite the location, he had an opportunity to stamp his own identity on the restaurant, filling it with front of house staff who would not look out of place on his TV show.

But Oliver's real move into the restaurant business came in the surprising form of the Fifteen chains.

Why surprising? Given the success that Oliver had enjoyed in the UK and around the world by this point, you would expect him to

capitalize on his fame by opening restaurants that
would heap spade loads of money into his
already bulging coffers. But Fifteen was a   **Oliver's real move into**
social venture, set up by Oliver as a vehi- **the restaurant business**
cle to train disadvantaged young peo-   **came in the surprising**
ple for a career in catering. It was (and is) **form of the Fifteen**
run as a commercial venture that has to   **chains**
pay for itself but the profits are reinvested
rather than taken by Oliver as dividends.

In fact, rather than earning money, Fifteen continued to be a drain
on Oliver's finances for many years. In 2007, journalists swooped
on the published accounts of Sweet as Candy, the company set
up by Oliver to manage his affairs and channel his revenues. Figures filed by the company showed a sharp fall in profits with Oliver
taking a dividend of £900,000 compared with £2.5m the previous
year. According to the company, the decline in both the profitability of the Oliver Empire and its owner's dividend was due to cash
being diverted to keep Fifteen up and running.

Looked at from another perspective, Fifteen has done Oliver no
harm whatsoever. For one thing, the project got him back on the
small screen. The corporation became concerned about Oliver's
relationship with Sainsbury's when he was signed to star in a campaign for the supermarket giant in 2000, but the BBC was less than
happy about the similarities between the content of his TV series
and the style of the Sainsbury ads and eventually the corporation
decided not to recommission his show.

Fifteen was his route back to mainstream television, with Channel
4 this time following his efforts to train a disparate group of young
people in the series *Jamie's Kitchen*. Since then, Oliver has continued to put his own money into Fifteen while overseeing an expan-

sion of the concept. Thanks to franchising agreements, branches of the restaurant are now open in London, Cornwall, Amsterdam and Melbourne. Indelibly associated with Oliver it has had an immensely beneficial effect on the public perception of Oliver the man, the idealist and the entrepreneur.

HIT THE HIGH STREET

With Fifteen firmly established on the UK (and international) restaurant map, Oliver has set his sights on establishing a fully commercial restaurant chain dubbed Jamie's Italian.

Anyone who has paid any attention to Oliver will know that he is a huge fan of Italian food and the philosophy that lies behind it: of rustic food and simple ingredients, with restaurants being centres of the community. As the Jamie's Italian website puts it: The aim is to create 'neighbourhood venues, inspired by the Italian table where people relax, share and enjoy each other's company.'

To date, Jamie's Italian restaurants have been opened in Oxford, Bath, Kingston-upon-Thames, Brighton and Canary Wharf in London's Docklands. More are scheduled for the future, including branches in Dubai, Hong Kong and across Asia.

Sitting neatly alongside the Italian restaurant chain are Oliver's Recipease food and kitchen shops, located in Clapham (London) and Brighton. Given Oliver's role as Britain's most popular food educator, it should probably surprise no one that the concept behind the stores is to encourage more people to experiment with food and try out new recipes.

A great many specialist food shops would claim to do the same thing, but Recipease has a few novel features up its sleeve. The starting point is the high quality ingredients required to create food the Jamie Oliver way, but shoppers can also access tips and advice from an onsite chef. Those who book can collect their ingredients pre-prepared or attend themed food parties. Meanwhile, the truly lazy can take advantage of a range of Jamie Oliver ready meals, boxed and ready to go. The lifestyle angle is covered too, with a range of Oliver-branded kitchenware and utensils.

Talking to the *London Evening Standard* in January 2009, Oliver said, 'I've wanted to create something special like this for a long time, something which offers the support and solutions in the neighbourhood that people need these days as so many people were never taught to cook at home or in school.[4]

EXPERIMENT

So, Oliver has been willing to stretch his personal brand into a broad range of areas – some more obvious than others. No one would bat an eyelid at the prospect of an Oliver magazine featuring a mix of recipes and articles. *Jamie* is that magazine and its launch contributed to an overall rise in sales of home and cookery magazines in the recession-hit first half of 2009. However, it has been criticized as an ego trip, and many find its focus on Oliver, Jools and their lifestyle does carry a whiff of self-importance and pretension. But it has proved popular, at home and internationally.

Kitchenware was another obvious avenue and if you'd like a piece of Jamie in the most important room in the house, there's a wide range of goods available: Oliver branded cookware – including saucepans – and the Flavour Shaker, his own invention, are widely available. You can also find his name on a range of ceramics and barbecue equipment. On the food front, he also has his own range of pasta sauces, herbs and cooking oils. Oliver's expansion into retail has been facilitated by strategic partnerships with major industry players such as Tefal (saucepans), William Levene (DKB), Royal Worcester (ceramics) and Merison (outdoor equipment).

Less obviously Oliver also worked with Wallace and Gromit creators Aardman animation on Little J, an animated TV series featuring a cartoon Oliver on a quest to become a great chef. Also somewhere on the left field is 'What's Cooking', a Nintendo DS game that takes Oliver's educational and cookery skills firmly into the digital age. Meanwhile, a partnership with mobile content company Inventa has seen Oliver appearing on the screens of 3G broadband mobile phones. We've come a long way since Fanny Craddock!

THE GOLDEN RULES OF BRAND EXTENSION

In extending his personal brand across a range of media channels and business opportunities, Oliver has followed a tried and tested route pursued by businesses of all sizes in search of higher revenues and increased profits. To put it simply, he has used the strength of his reputation – the strength of his brand – to diversify and for the most part he's done so very successfully.

For those who get it right, diversification is a great way to grow a business, not least because it allows you to sell a lot more products to wider markets. Think of it this way. Whether you're selling cookbooks or refrigerators there will come a time when the market for your particular product is saturated.

That in itself needn't be anything close to disastrous. Let's say your business has hit a peak selling 100,000 fridges a year. If that figure made you a profit in 2009 the chances are it will continue to do so in 2011, so you don't have any immediate worries about financial security.

But what happens when a new manufacturer steps into the market with a product so good that it cuts your sales in half? Suddenly the figures don't look so good and the future is very uncertain. The truth is that once sales of a particular product hit a peak, the next step is often a slow or sharp decline.

So what can you do? Well, if you happen to be a TV chef you can write more cookbooks and hope that your audience will buy, say, two a year, rather than one. If you sell fridges you can update your models and continue to sell to the market. In terms of business growth strategy, what you're doing here is stepping up your production and marketing efforts essentially to sell more of the same product to an existing customer base.

A second strategy is to take the products you're known for – in Oliver's case cookbooks and TV programmes – and reach a new audience. Oliver has done that successfully throughout his career. Since the early days of *The Naked Chef*, his television work has been sold to overseas TV networks, giving him a huge and receptive international audience.

And it's a route that a lot of businesses take. The home market may be saturated, but if you have a product that will appeal to buyers in France, Germany, Australia or the US and you can successfully market your company in those countries, then you can continue to grow sales for years to come. And expansion overseas can provide a way to buck recessionary trends. The bathroom fittings company that struggles in a stagnant UK housing market may well find a much more receptive market in Dubai or India.

Equally, Oliver has found a new audience at home as his screen persona has developed from mouthy kitchen iconoclast to a grown up campaigner for quality food and animal welfare. This is really a case of selling more by extending the appeal of the brand. You take a product that appeals to one audience and market to another by changing the way it is perceived. Take the Filofax – the aforementioned icon of the eighties. For years it languished as a specialist organizational tool for military officers. In the eighties, it was rebranded as a must-have status symbol for young urban professionals. And with a new market to conquer, the new owners saw sales rising to undreamed of levels.

To put it simply, he has used the strength of his reputation – the strength of his brand – to diversify and for the most part he's done so very successfully

But Oliver hasn't stopped there. Those who wish to grow their fortunes rapidly have two more strategies at their disposal – selling new products to the existing customer base and (the more difficult one to pull off) selling new products into previously tapped markets.

Oliver has certainly had a good stab at the first of those. His range of branded products – kitchenware, sauces, etc – has found a receptive market amongst those who have consumed his cookery books, as have his restaurants and shops. Meanwhile, he has attempted to reach both new and existing groups of fans and customers through his video game and animation ventures.

Diversification isn't solely about profits – it also has a defensive side. Oliver's career in television has been stellar, but as his early setback with the BBC illustrated, there are no guarantees of continued success. The programme that is popular today could be dropped tomorrow if audiences fall or the production companies want a fresh face. And without the support of television, book sales also take a hit. Diversification offers a degree of protection. If Oliver's TV career ended tomorrow, the restaurants and Recipease stores would still be there, and once established in their communities they have the potential to take on a momentum of their own. Similarly, if Oliver's Fresh One production company can detach itself from its origins as the chef's own vehicle, it has the potential to remain profitable for a long, long time, even after its founder has moved on to other things.

Brand extension has its risks. Using an existing trading name, brand or even a personal reputation to launch new products makes it easier to win customers. For instance, anyone launching a range of kitchenware under an entirely new name would probably struggle if Jamie Oliver's counterparts were sitting on the shelf.

That's not to say the brand X products wouldn't sell. If they're well designed, competitively priced and have that certain something that sets them apart, they could well go on to become the next big thing. However, building a reputation (and sales) will take time. On the other hand, launch a Jamie Oliver range and you have a captive audience.

But there are risks. For one thing, a poor product – or even a good one that somehow fails to ignite the public's imagination – may damage the parent brand if it generates a negative response. That was a lesson learned in the 1990s by the companies that made up the Independent Television (ITV) group. Harnessing their reins to the revolution in digital television, they launched the ONdigital terrestrial television platform. It wasn't a bad service by any means but as ITV struggled to compete with satellite operator Sky, it failed to generate sufficient revenue to justify the investment and satisfy shareholders. The ultimate closure of the service damaged the parent ITV brand in the eyes of the public (and perhaps more importantly advertisers and shareholders) for years to come.

Then there is the ever-present danger that you can stretch the brand too far. This has been an occasional problem for Richard Branson and his Virgin empire. Always spoiling for a knockout fight with the corporates, Branson has established the Virgin logo as a 'challenger brand'. In essence, this means that at the heart of Virgin's identity is the fact that it is ready, willing and very able to take on major corporates in just about any consumer sector and provide a livelier, hipper and sometimes better value service than established rivals. Thus we see the 'V' on trains, aircraft, soft drinks, alcoholic drinks, financial products, cable services and mobile phones. But Branson doesn't always succeed. People may love Virgin Airways, but Virgin Cola has failed to give Coca-Cola or Pepsi too many sleepless nights.

Oliver has been much more conservative about the use of his name. Recognizing that key to successful brand extension is an understanding of what his name means to a domestic and international audience, he has, by and large, expanded his empire through careful steps into areas of business that are closely related to his status as chef and educator. Video games and animated TV series may push the envelope a little but for the most part he has stuck to his knitting, and avoided the hubris of believing that the name Jamie Oliver will sell anything from fast cars to boiler parts. Even his TV production company, although it has used a range of presenters, has tended to focus on themes of food and drink.

All that may change, but for the moment the Oliver empire has pulled off the trick of diversifying into new businesses while also remaining tightly focused. It's a strategy that has proved hugely successful.

EXTEND YOUR BRAND

Jamie Oliver has built a formidable business empire without taking undue risks with his hard won reputation. The public like and trust the character they see on TV and Oliver has become a bankable brand. As his business empire has grown he has ensured that all his ventures chime with his public image. The lessons are:

- **Take control of your affairs.** By negotiating his own royalties on books related to *The Naked Chef* series, Jamie indicated that he was a man who sought to control his own destiny. His decision to form an independent production company to produce his own shows has allowed him a huge amount of freedom to develop the ideas that have kept him in the public eye.
- **Build the business around the values people associate with you.** Throughout his TV career, Oliver has fostered the image of a straight talking, vocal, but passionate advocate of good food and ethical practices. His philosophies about the relationship between food and community are reflected in ventures such as Jamie's Italian and Recipease. Meanwhile, the Fifteen chain stands testimony to his ethical stance.

- **Stick to your knitting.** Oliver's expertise is focused on food and cooking. His business ventures reflect that.
- **Partner with others.** Oliver has always sought to hire talented people to run and work for his companies. Equally important, he has extended his brand (and his public persona) through partnerships with organizations as diverse as Sainsbury's, Tefal and Aardman animation.
- **Plan for the future.** By diversifying into a range of ventures, Oliver has created a stable business platform for himself that is capable of surviving should his TV celebrity begin to fade.
- **Ride the lifestyle wave.** Oliver's success is based on the transitory medium of television, communicating not only recipes but a cool, healthy and enviable way of life. By creating a demand for that lifestyle, he has also created demand for the products, restaurants and shops that can provide it. Those products and services are available under the Oliver brand.

3

BUILD ON WHAT YOU'RE GOOD AT

As businessman, TV celebrity and best-selling author, Jamie Oliver has covered a huge amount of ground in a public career that's little more than a decade old. He's pushed the boundaries of popular food television, launched a string of businesses, established himself as a formidable political lobbyist and helped to turn around the fortunes of a major supermarket.

But here's the thing. Whether filming a reality TV show highlighting the problems of poverty and poor nutrition, chatting with prime ministers about policy or negotiating with business partners about a new line of products, he's always stayed pretty close to his own comfort zone. Put simply, food is what Oliver knows about. His entire professional life has centred on his skills as a chef and his understanding of the role that food plays in all our lives. From that core competency he's built a multi-faceted business empire.

That's probably not surprising. Food was in his blood and the pub/restaurant trade was the family business. Food was a route to financial independence. Like his father before him, Oliver finished school with little to show in the way of formal qualifications. But what he lacked on paper, he made up for in ambition. Spurred on by parents who had no desire to see their son join the ranks of the undereducated unemployed, he wanted to do something with his life. Aside from an outside chance of making the big time with his band, Scarlet Division, a career in the restaurant trade was an obvious choice, it would give him access to decently paid jobs. Maybe in time it would also provide him with an opportunity to work for himself and build a business.

In that respect, the course of his early life was not surprising. If he came from a different family background his choice of vocation might have been car mechanic, hairdresser or any one of a number of trades that require hard work and application over academic achievement. But by the time he waved goodbye to the kitchens of the family restaurant and began studying for a chef's diploma at Westminster Kingsway College, the parameters for his future life were firmly in place.

He studied for a chef's diploma at Westminster Kingsway – a course that provided him with all the basic knowledge required to work as a chef in the catering industry. It covered not only the cooking but also the serving of food, hygiene, health and safety, and a huge amount of related background knowledge. When he qualified, he was a food professional. That didn't mean he could walk into any kitchen in the land and assume a senior role – that would require time on the job.

But within Oliver's chosen trade, there was plenty of scope to forge a successful career When he began his course at Westminster Kingsway, the era of the celebrity chef had already begun so the idea of a stellar career running and owning a chain of restaurants was certainly not outlandish.

Oliver may well have looked to two earlier graduates of Westminster Kingsway, Ainsley Harriott and Antony Worrall Thompson as examples of what could be achieved. Both were successful chefs with TV careers. Perhaps more importantly, they had off-screen careers as successful restaurateurs. They had shown what could be possible.

CORE COMPETENCIES

Success in any walk of life generally relies on having a range of core competencies upon which to draw. A great musician is likely to remain unsung outside the bedroom unless he or she has a range of self-promotional and networking skills to deploy. Later, as their career takes off, he or she is going to need a whole new set of skills to stay in the game and continue to be successful: the ability to move forward, keeping the material fresh; to draw on new influences and assimilate them; the ability to strike good deals – or at least understand the deals managers, promoters, agents and record companies are cooking up – and the ability to partner with the right people.

He started chopping vegetables and progressed to cooking in his teens. Perhaps more importantly he spent time in the company of chefs and got a taste for the life

You could apply the same criteria to garage mechanics, hairdressers, plumbers, builders, electricians or chefs. A vocational skill is a gateway to employment but in order to take your career further you need a few more ingredients on the plate. Despite a lack of academic achievement, Oliver quickly made it obvious to all that came into contact with him that he had core competencies in abundance.

Aside from his knowledge of food and cookery, the greatest of these was an ability to communicate. There was a public and a private side to this. As a TV presenter, his was the gift of the motormouthed food enthusiast who could both inspire viewers and impart information. Away from the cameras, Oliver has a reputation for being able to talk to just about anyone on an equal footing and (where necessary) get his own way.

When Sainsbury's approached him to do a series of television ads, rather than simply saying yes, taking the money and submitting himself to scripts created by the creative agency, Oliver negotiated with CEO Sir Peter Davis. The result was a series of ads that drew on the strengths of Oliver's existing TV persona. Communication – and in particular the ability to inspire and persuade others – is a vital skill for entrepreneurs.

Oliver himself tends to stress the importance of hard work in his success story and he can be a taskmaster when it comes to other people. Perhaps equally importantly he gets excited about new ventures and works hard on every project to ensure that is has the maximum chance of success. But that excitement is coupled with an instinctive ability to understand not only the potential of his appeal but also its limits. As we saw in the last chapter, he has extended his brand aggressively while remaining cautious about overstretching its core values to an uncomfortable degree.

HOW FAR CAN YOU STRETCH?

In a parallel universe, you might turn on a TV and find Jamie Oliver hosting a chat show, discussing movies on a late night review programme or endorsing a financial services product during an ad break. In that same universe you might walk into your local branch of Marks & Spencer and find Oliver-designed hoodies in the Autograph range.

But in this universe, Oliver has pretty much stuck to what he knows. Yes, he has extended his business through a range of TV styles and widening of branded products, restaurants and retail ventures, but food is at the core of everything he does.

It doesn't necessarily have to be this way. The world is full of TV celebrities, sports stars, rock musicians and Page Three models that have been happy to move between genres with promiscuous ease or endorse products that have only a tenuous relationship to their public personas.

Take the omnipresent TV presenter, Adrian Chiles as an example. Armed with an English literature degree he later trained as a journalist and began his working life as a radio sports reporter. Since then, he's had stints presenting *The Financial World Tonight* (Radio 4), *Working Lunch* (a BBC TV business programme), and now *The One Show*, a prime-time magazine chat show. In between, he also fronted the BBC's Olympics coverage in 2008.

Chiles is by no means alone. Stephen Fry has moved on from sketch comedy to a variety of TV and film roles that range from serious acting to documentaries on AIDs and endangered wildlife, while also finding time to write novels and an autobiography, and front a new radio series.

You can also find numerous examples of celebrities stretching their brand on the product marketing front. Witness the latest venture from England rugby star Lawrence Dallaglio. In 2009, he launched his own range of pasta sauces, initially bound for the shelves of Waitrose supermarket. The British public can now choose between sauces bearing the image of Jamie Oliver (chef), Lloyd Grossman (chef) and Lawrence Dallaglio (a sportsman celebrated for his skills with a peculiarly-shaped ball).

So why would Dallaglio choose to take this route, rather than stick to a sporting theme and endorsing or designing rugby boots or trainers? Well, for one thing, the celebrity sauce market is reputedly worth around £80m in the UK, so it's a lucrative pond to dip your toes into. Secondly, Dallaglio has positioned the sauce as a healthy choice, an attribute that ties in with his sporting past. Crucially, also present in the marketing mix is his Italian heritage.

Talking to *Real Business* magazine, brand consultant Robert Bean – who hooked Dallaglio up with sauce manufacturer Sacla Clare Blampied, enthused about the potential for the product to reach a market on the back of the rugby player's fame. 'The rugby fraternity will love it,' he says. 'Mums will try it, kids will ask for it and blokes, especially those who are reluctant in the kitchen, will also buy it because you have this man's man saying cooking is OK.'[1]

But in this universe, Oliver has pretty much stuck to what he knows best ... food is at the core of everything he does

Dallaglio's venture illustrates that celebrity brand extension can be an elastic thing. Sports stars aren't limited to boots, sweatshirts and kit bags. They can also do a nice line in marketing razors, leisurewear, aftershave or indeed pasta sauce. Thus, no one will bat an eyelid when pop/rock icon Bryan Ferry 'designs' a range of clothing for the Marks & Spencer Autograph range. Nor are we surprised to see equestrian clothing marketed in the name of Jordan, or Bollywood actress and *Big Brother* housemate Shilpa Shetty launching a range of ready meals.

Elsewhere, you'll find Britney Spears giving her name to a fragrance and rock musician Sheryl Crow launching a line of jeans for the US market and our very own Emma Watson (Hermione from the Harry

Potter movies) collaborating with People Tree, a 'sustainable fair trade fashion brand'.

Indeed, sometimes it seems that everyone who has enjoyed more than fifteen minutes of fame is on the look out for a venture through which to capitalize on their celebrity.

The path to product endorsement is well trodden. The up-and-coming celebrity hires an agent cum brand manager so handle his or her business affairs. The agent talks to manufacturers or marketing specialists on the lookout for a celebrity figurehead. The next thing you know, you have a new perfume, clothing range or signature watch hitting the shelves.

There are some golden rules though. Bryan Ferry is a musician and songwriter first and foremost, but his image has been built around a love of elegant clothes, tempered with an art-school sensibility. Thus, it doesn't require too much of a leap of imagination to see a generation of Ferry fans looking with more than passing interest at his contribution to the M&S clothing racks.

You'll also find David Beckham in M&S in the form of his DB clothing range. As with Ferry it's the associations that matter here. Beckham is primarily a footballer but as his fame has grown, he has become increasingly associated with the world of high fashion and an opulent lifestyle. So, once again, clothing is a natural home for the Beckham brand.

You might argue that Jamie Oliver could easily go down the same route. Certainly mention of his name conjures up a range of associations that go way beyond food. There are the scooters, the clothes, the fashionable lifestyle, and his love of music to name but four. In sartorial terms, Oliver is no Bryan Ferry, but it's not hard to imagine, for example, a collection of surf clothing bearing his name.

So why has Oliver so far stuck closely to the subject that he knows best? TV chefs have – by and large – chosen to extend their brands within the culinary arena rather than branching out into unfamiliar territory. Witness Gordon Ramsay. Like Oliver he has pushed the boundaries of 'on the box' cookery to encompass the reality TV format of *Ramsay's Kitchen Nightmares*, *Hell's Kitchen* and *The F Word*. Outside the studio, he runs successful restaurants and he's put his name to a range of products, including a kitchenware range sold in Argos and chinaware sold in John Lewis. On the endorsement front he's appeared in commercials for Gordon's Gin (something of an obvious choice). So, as with Oliver, the dominant theme of his business activities is food and drink related products.

In building on what he knows, Oliver has successfully created a food lifestyle brand and business that is more than the sum of its parts while staying true to the original unspoken deal between Oliver and the public

There's a pretty good reason why TV chefs focus their brand extensions around their core competency. Unlike, say, a footballer, a model or a rock musician, the skills they impart on TV along with the associated kitchen paraphernalia can be easily packaged into readily marketable branded products.

Think of it this way. Bryan Ferry can sell records and DVDs but he can't 'package' the talent that makes those records appealing. His singing voice and song writing talent are his and his alone – they are not transferable except as recorded artefacts.

The TV chef on the other hand can easily package his core skill, primarily through the medium of the recipe book and the instructional DVD, but there are plenty of other avenues to choose from. You can experience directly Oliver's approach to cooking by eating in his restaurants, by mixing one of his sauces into a pasta meal or by purchasing some prepared ingredients from a Recipease shop. And by buying into his kitchenware you can enjoy a taste of the associated lifestyle. It's an illusion of course. A complete set of Tefal/Jamie Oliver saucepans in the cupboard won't transport the consumer to a trendy London pad or a country retreat (as seen in the TV series) but it does provide some kind of psychological link with the chef's enviable lifestyle.

What's more, Oliver's food-focused empire is infinitely expandable. Yes, there's probably a limit to the number of pasta sauces he can sell in any given year, but when you look to the restaurant business he has a world to conquer. If a restaurant succeeds in Bath or Oxford, the chances are it will succeed in dozens of similar British towns. If food flies out of a Jamie's Italian kitchen in Hong Kong, there's no reason why the brand shouldn't be equally successful in Japan, Singapore or any of the Asian countries where the chef already has a high profile.

So, in that respect, there isn't any need to take risks with the brand or to fall back on secondary associations (such as Oliver the surfer who drives a VW Camper Van or Oliver the Rock Fan). As far as business expansion goes, the cookery/food theme still has enormous potential.

And there's a second factor at work. The key to Oliver's success lies in the trust that he's built up since his earliest days on the TV. Oliver is a food professional who spent years honing his skills and he is also passionate about his chosen career. His methods may seem slapdash but those who appreciate his work know that he learnt all the rules of cookery before he started to break them. More important, those who buy his books and watch the TV shows know that a commitment to using quality ingredients lies at the heart of his cooking philosophy.

So the expectation is that a Jamie Oliver pasta sauce will reflect that commitment to quality, with the ingredients and manufacturing process subject to the great man's 'hands on' interest and seal of approval. Whether consumers would feel the same about a Jamie Oliver signature watch or hoodie is an open question.

And in the end it all comes down to a simple fact. Oliver knows about food and nutrition. By staying within that universe he can talk authoritatively and remain firmly in the driving seat across all his business ventures. If he were to extend his brand into areas where he has less expertise, it would be much harder for him to retain the same authority.

CONNECT ACROSS THE MEDIA

In building on what he knows, Oliver has successfully created a food lifestyle brand and business that is more than the sum of its parts, while staying true to the original unspoken deal between Oliver and the public.

Ubiquity is the key to its success. Oliver connects with his audience – TV viewers and paying consumers across multiple points of contact. These include television, bookshops and libraries, restaurants, retail chains, supermarkets, his own store and last (but by no means least) the Internet. In addition to selling himself or his products, he is also communicating across a broad range of media – television, DVDs, books, magazines, computer games and web pages and blogs.

More customer touch points mean increased opportunities to build the brand and sell products. At one level it's the classic cross-sell. Those who've bought into the television shows may well choose a Jamie's Italian restaurant for a special night out and splash out on his kitchenware when the time comes to refurbish the kitchen.

But there's also an opportunity to win new customers. Those who've avoided the TV shows and books – perhaps deterred by the copious references to 'luvvly jubbly' and 'pukka' food – may none-theless try out the restaurants, either out of curiosity or because they've heard the food is good.

The range of media broadens the appeal and widens the demo-graphic. For those who don't fancy the books, the DVDs provide a means to bring a little bit of Oliver's culinary magic into the home. Meanwhile, the Cook Up video game reaches out to the digital generation.

BRINGING IT ALL TOGETHER

The strength and clarity of Oliver's brand proposition becomes clear when you visit Oliver's main website, jamieoliver.com.

In technical terms the site has a lot to do. As a centralized point of contact for all things Oliver it covers a lot of bases. Not surprisingly, there is a huge amount of information about Oliver's TV shows, books and DVD releases. Indeed, in the unlikely event of a Martian visitor arriving on Earth for the first time with the express purpose of catching up with the chef's entire back catalogue, the website would probably be the first port of call.

Then we have a résumé of Oliver's campaigns and social ventures, from Fifteen/*Jamie's Kitchen* through *Jamie's School Dinners* and *Ministry of Food* to *Jamie's Fowl Dinners* and *Jamie Saves our Bacon*. There is more here than a few lines on each campaign. Navigate through the increasingly complex menu system and you'll find snippets of background research, recipes, manifestos for change and updates on the progress of each of the initiatives. You'll also find information on his Italian restaurants, Recipease and his party plan ventures.

There's transactional purpose to all this. The casual browser with an interest in, say, the *Ministry of Food* campaign, also has the opportunity to buy the book of the series (complete with cost-effective simple recipes) by clicking on a link. The same technique is replicated throughout the site. JamieOliver.com is not just about information; it is also about e-commerce.

And that's true even of the community sections. Oliver has been rightly commended for his use of social media links within his site. In addition to forums where fans of Oliver and his shows can chat and exchange recipes there is also a personal 'blog' function, which allows any registered user to start up a personal journal. It's a lively and well-used facility. Features such as recipe shares and competitions help to maintain interest and drive repeat visits.

And when design agency Thinkflow Interactive were asked to design a transactional website for Oliver's new line of JME Lifestyle Collection products, one key strategy was a close integration between the Jamieoliver.com site, including its community pages, and the JME Lifestyle collection transactional opportunities. Put simply, information forum and blog pages are seeded with links to the JME Lifestyle products, with the links themselves placed according to the context of the site and its subject matter. The concept is simple. By contributing to a forum, or browsing through pages relating to school dinners, visitors to the site reveal something about themselves and their own interests. This knowledge can be used to sell products to those same visitors. [2]

Jamieoliver.com is not the chef's only point of online contact. You'll also find standalone websites dedicated to Fifteen, Recipease and Jamie's Italian. Elsewhere, you'll find Oliver on Twitter, Myspace, Facebook and Bebo.

But it's Jamieoliver.com that brings all his interests together within a unified whole. Oliver has often stressed that his commercial activities exist separately from his TV and campaigning work and to some extent that is true. But as the site demonstrates, when Oliver generates interest in a particular subject via a TV show or campaigning statement, there is also ample opportunity to drive sales.

STICK TO WHAT YOU'RE GOOD AT

Jamie Oliver has succeeded in creating a multi-faceted business while continuing to focus on the subject that he knows best – food. Here's how he's done it:

- **Get proper training.** Thanks to growing up in a gastro pub, Oliver was steeped in restaurant and catering business from an early age. But he knew the value of training. At the age of sixteen he enrolled at the Westminster Kingsway College on a professional chef's diploma course. When he emerged, he was well on his way to becoming a food professional.
- **Build on your competencies.** Aside from cookery, Oliver's greatest attribute was an ability to communicate. By combining his knowledge of food with the gift of the gab he quickly demonstrated an ability to both entertain a TV audience and impart information with authority.
- **Sell what you understand.** From pasta sauces and herbs to the meals prepared in Fifteen and Jamie's Italian, Oliver fully understands the products and services that are sold under his name. And while his brand has stretched a little in recent times – for example marketing the JME Lifestyle connection – his chosen markets lie close to his core expertise.
- **Recognize the scope of your chosen business sector.** While choosing to focus for the most part on products, services and media in the arena of food and lifestyle, Oliver has succeeded in identifying huge potential for expansion.

- **Cross-selling.** By sticking to what he knows best, Oliver has created opportunities to cross-sell. Fans of the TV shows buy his books, eat in his restaurants and buy his kitchenware. The range of Jamie Oliver endorsed products on offer to the consumer make sense – they all link to his background in food.

- **Use multiple points of contact.** By extending his food brand across a range of shops, restaurants, and media outlets, Oliver has expanded his audience size and its demographic. In addition to traditional media (books, magazines etc.) his use of social media networks like Twitter and Facebook help him attract a younger audience. Even the digital gaming market is catered for via his Cook Up title for Nintendo DS.

- **Use new media.** Oliver's website demonstrates that despite the multi-faceted nature of his businesses, he has a clear brand proposition. United by bright graphics and text, the site brings together his TV work, books, campaigns and business products together under one roof. Different aspects of his activities are cross-referenced and the factual information gathered on visitors to the site drives e-commerce sales.

4

REMEMBER THE
SOCIAL DIMENSION

Who would have Adam and Eve'd it? When Jamie Oliver first burst onto Britain's television screens in the guise of the 'naked chef' he seemed to epitomize the brash self-confidence of a young man determined to seize more than his fair share of all the good things life had to offer. Good food, a trendy lifestyle, a beautiful girlfriend, a growing personal fortune. As he slid down that spiral staircase – a trademark of *The Naked Chef* series – it seemed that all these things were his for the taking.

At that stage in his career, few critics or even fans would have detected – or even tried to detect – a social conscience. All that mattered was that Oliver was a breath of fresh air in the world of TV cooking and a hugely entertaining communicator.

Fast forward to 2002. Channel 4 is airing *Jamie's Kitchen*, a show in which Oliver is leading an attempt to mould a diverse group of unemployed teenagers into a team of trained chefs, capable of producing food for the tables of a top quality London restaurant. Totally unlike *The Naked Chef*, this was a show with a very different vibe. As Oliver explained in the introduction to the book of the series, after five years of success, he was ready to 'give something back'.

But he did more than make a token gesture via a TV series. The training initiative that he launched to rejuvenate his career is still going strong today, centred around the Fifteen Restaurant. That in itself would be an achievement, but Oliver also succeeded in raising the profile of Britain's 'social ventures' – businesses that exist to deliver social benefits rather than enriching the founders.

Jamie's Kitchen was a show with a point to make. In the accompanying book of the same name, Oliver acknowledges that in terms of academic achievement he was far from the 'brightest banana in the bunch'. Having left school at 16 with just two higher level GSCEs to his name, he was pretty close to the bottom of the academic heap. So much so that some people would have written him off. Five years later, he was fronting a TV show, penning bestselling cookery books and beginning to accumulate a fortune. He was living proof that you can't write anyone off. Maybe he didn't have ten good GCSEs, but he had the fire of ambition burning in his belly and a willingness to work hard to achieve his goals. Those qualities had been crucial to his success and a key part of the thinking behind *Jamie's Kitchen*. Oliver wanted to demonstrate that with sufficient determination and application, and the chance to prove it, anyone can forge a successful and satisfying career.

The series proved to be hugely successful piece of reality TV, but it was underpinned by a much more wide-ranging project. Oliver had become committed not simply to helping a single group of teenagers to transcend problems of alcoholism and drug abuse and build successful careers in the catering industry in front of the camera; his long term aim was to create a sustainable business that would continue to train disadvantaged young people, long after the tapes of *Jamie's Kitchen* had been safely consigned to the archives.

The idea was a simple one. The Fifteen Foundation would be set up as a charity dedicated to training unemployed teenagers – some of them genuinely disadvantaged – to work in the catering industry. Meanwhile, the Fifteen Restaurant would be run on commercial grounds. Staffed largely by graduates and trainees from the programme, it would offer a top class service and food. The profits would be ploughed back into the training programme rather than going to shareholders but, in the long term, profitability was essential if Fifteen was to succeed.

That profitability depended on the quality of the experience. From the customer's perspective the laudable aims of Fifteen would mean little if the food was poor or the service indifferent. So Fifteen was not in the business of offering free rides. To graduate from the training programme, participants would have to show themselves capable of working in a high quality restaurant with all the pressures that entails.

Fifteen wasn't established to make Oliver rich – in fact it was a drain on his resources for some years – but the story of how the project was implemented provides a neat illustration of how the entrepreneurial mind works.

TURN AN IDEA INTO REALITY

As with many business ventures, Fifteen started as a small idea that nagged away at Oliver for a number of years. As he told chat show host Michael Parkinson in 2002, the origin of the project was a conversation that took place shortly after Oliver and wife Jools moved to London. One of Jools' friends was working with disadvantaged kids in Brighton. 'They were very erratic, quite aggressive kids', he recalled. 'The only time they really shone was then they were taking apart a scooter or cooking, because they could eat it.'

That observation planted a seed in Oliver's mind and as his own career developed, the idea of Fifteen began to take on more substance. The restaurant would be the hub of the operation, but trainees would be sent to work in the kitchens of some of Britain's most celebrated restaurants and hotels. Mentors would be on hand to guide the trainees and the whole experience would allow the teenagers taking part to excel in a rapidly expanding sector.

To make the project work, Oliver drew on his own extensive list of friends and contacts in the catering world, including his one time mentor, Italian chef Gennaro Contaldo and former employers Rose Gray and Ruth Rogers of the River Café Restaurant.

The next stage was recruiting trainees, a task that was carried out by putting out alerts through job centres and radio stations. It was a trawling operation that produced around 1500 potential candidates, a list that had to be shaved down to around sixty people.

Oliver has stressed that he wasn't necessarily looking for disadvantaged teenagers for the programme. Problems with drugs, alcohol or homelessness certainly wouldn't exclude candidates but neither was a colourful background or difficult story any guarantee of a place. Oliver was seeking to make a TV programme out of the venture, but as he told Michael Parkinson, he wasn't searching specifically for 'problem kids' to feed the TVs appetite for drama. 'Most of the kids we chose weren't disadvantaged. They were just regular unemployed kids who I felt had a spark in their eyes', he said.

Oliver also succeeded in raising the profile of Britain's 'social ventures' – businesses that exist to deliver social benefits rather than enriching the founders

The concept was turned down by the BBC but when the series aired on Channel 4 there was no shortage of drama. Some of it centred around the kids themselves as they struggled to comply with the disciplines of a working day, the pressure of commercial kitchens and an intense training regime. But much of it focused on the challenges faced by Oliver in making the project work. Meanwhile, as a kind sub-plot, the strains placed on the Olivers' marriage by the venture were also depicted on screen.

Bringing all this together required a huge amount of energy and commitment and, while the driving force behind Fifteen appears to have been a genuine desire to make a difference, the idea would not have got off the ground without Oliver's ability to organize and motivate. For the truth is, ideas are worth very little unless followed up by action. Most of us have moments of inspiration where we come up with concepts that could change the world or make as multimillionaires. Very often those ideas are quickly forgotten or we simply fail to follow through with solid plans. Natural entrepreneurs, on the other hand, work out a route map that will take them from raw concept to workable venture. The *Jamie's Kitchen*/Fifteen plan was almost certainly born out of enlightened altruism rather than self-interest, but its success is testimony to the fact that Oliver was more than just another TV chef. If not quite yet an entrepreneur, he was certainly an organizational force to be reckoned with.

Fifteen wasn't established to make Oliver rich – in fact it was a drain on his resources for some years – but the story of how project was implemented provides a neat illustration of how the entrepreneurial mind works

MAKING A SOCIAL VENTURE WORK

In establishing the Fifteen Foundation as both a charity and enterprise operating on commercial principals, Oliver was joining a growing army of 'social entrepreneurs'.

According to figures published by Britain's Department for Business Industry and Skills (BIS) there are more than 50,000 social enterprises operating in the United Kingdom at the moment, employing more than half a million people. [1]

The scope of the not-for-profit business sector is huge. Some have global concerns. For instance, the company behind bottled drinks company One Water ploughs its profits into the supply of clean water technology for the developing world. Others are locally focused – perhaps providing training or work experience for the disadvantaged in a particular city or district. The common factor is that social ventures generate income and pay wages rather than relying on donations and the work of volunteers. Equally important, they either give away their profits to good causes or reinvest them in their own programmes. As defined by BIS, a social enterprise is a business with primarily social objectives.

But, like any business, social ventures have to pay their way and arguably those who establish and run them have to be as entrepreneurial, committed and hands-on as any Richard Branson or Alan Sugar.

Oliver can certainly tick two out of the above boxes. In his own way he is certainly entrepreneurial and few would question his initial and ongoing commitment to the Fifteen project. But hands-on? With the *Jamie's Kitchen* series done and dusted, Oliver moved on to pastures new and in the next few years much of his missionary zeal was directed towards his high profile campaign to improve the quality of school dinners.

Equally, he has had commercial fish to fry. There were ads to make for Sainsbury's, restaurants to open, a new TV series in the pipeline, not to mention the launch of Oliver-branded food and kitchenware products. Arguably, *Jamie's Kitchen* and Fifteen turned Oliver into Britain's best known social entrepreneur, but he was also in the business of developing fully commercial projects and growing his own bank balance.

Fifteen has not withered on a neglected vine. By March 2009 just over 180 young people had signed on for traineeships with around half of that number completing the course. Meanwhile, London's Fifteen restaurant had been joined by franchises operating on similar principles in Cornwall, Melbourne and New York.

During that time Oliver's role within the organization has inevitably changed. As Fifteen's 2009 Social Report acknowledged: 'As Fifteen became stronger, he moved from hands-on operational involvement to a more strategic role as a board member of the foundation.'

As a trustee Oliver provides a guiding hand rather than the role of an operational manager. With the day-to-day running of Fifteen entrusted to front-of-house staff, and training put in the hands of professionals in the catering field, his role is increasingly one of inspirational figurehead.

As a trustee he has also played an important part in building an experienced management team. Among the key players was Fifteen's director Liam Black, founder of the Furniture Resource Centre, one of Britain's pioneering social enterprises.

Based in Liverpool, the FRC turned a small charity supplying council tenants with second-hand furniture into a fully-fledged not-for-profit business with a turnover of £5.5m. He joined the Fifteen Foundation with no direct experience of the restaurant trade. However, what he did bring was a strong sense of how the social enterprise model can work successfully to create employment and deliver positive social outcomes. A major part of his role was driving the expansion of the Fifteen brand to other franchised sites in the UK and overseas while ensuring that the underlying concept of the business wasn't lost in the transition.

Black signalled his intention to leave Fifteen in 2008, creating an opening for the venture's new chief executive, Penny Newman. Talking to *The Guardian* in 2009 she spoke of her plans to step up the scope of Fifteen's training operations: 'The nucleus of my vision for Fifteen is that we can become a training hub for the whole hotel industry, offering young people skills in every aspect of the restaurant, such as sourcing and procurement or front-of-house. So you don't need to want to become a chef in order to come through our programme', she said.[2]

So Oliver had to make a case. During the making of *School Dinners***, his researchers at the Fresh One production company were in overdrive**

Newman – formerly of The Body Shop and Fairtrade coffee company Cafédirect – admitted that she faced challenges. There was a need, she said, to raise revenues and profits at the all-important London restaurant. Equally, there was a clear need to rejuvenate the Fifteen brand.

Newman felt that although people may have known what Fifteen was before, they may not even be aware that the apprenticeship still existed. More importantly, she wanted to distinguish Fifteen as a brand in its own right.

As Newman's thoughts illustrate, the continuing association between Oliver and the venture he created represents something of a doubled-edged sword. On the plus side is the indisputable fact that without his energy and enthusiasm (and his financial backing) there would be no Fifteen. On the other hand, with Oliver no longer around, the restaurant business must now establish itself as an attractive destination in its own right. Book a table and the chances are that you won't catch a glimpse of the great man, so why choose Fifteen over any other London restaurant? The answer has to lie in the quality of both the food and customer service. As memories of the TV series fade, Fifteen must be able to stand on its own two feet. And, paradoxically, the Oliver association can be something of a handicap, if only because potential customers assume that it will always be fully booked up or that tables will only be available on unpopular nights of the week.

Securing the continued backing of sponsors is also a challenge. On taking over as chief executive, Penny Newman announced plans to forge new links with other players in the food industry, while simultaneously stepping up efforts to keep the work of the charity and quality of the restaurant at the forefront of both the public mind and that of potential corporate backers.

Newman believed that this would help them expand their work and help to refresh the Fifteen brand. By connecting with other food companies to develop more training schemes, she felt that this would help to provide more opportunities for young people to learn about the industry.

In Liam Black and Penny Newman, Fifteen has been lucky to secure people with the skills and experience to carry on where Oliver left off. In the case of Black his ambitious approach to growing the business of FRC put him in an ideal situation to expand the reach of Fifteen through domestic and overseas franchises while holding firm to Fifteen's founding principals.

Similarly, Penny Newman was appointed at a time when Fifteen's brand needed a shake-up and, with a background in marketing at Avon and Fabergé prior to her stints at The Body Shop and Cafédirect, she was ideally placed to deliver the necessary kick.

But there's a bigger point here. Whether a business is run for profit or exists to deliver a social benefit there will come a time when the founder moves on or shifts focus elsewhere. The key is to ensure that when that happens, the right people are waiting in the wings.

THE CAMPAIGN TRAIL

If the *Jamie's Kitchen* series and his ongoing commitment to Fifteen changed the public's perception of Oliver, then his next project both enhanced his status as a social campaigner and transformed him into a figure with genuine political clout.

That project centred on Oliver's passionate belief that the nation's children were being short changed when it came to the food served up to them in schools. In Oliver's view – and it was shared by many – the drive to bring catering costs down had resulted in a lunchtime diet of processed food with little or no nutritional value. Poor quality meat and sugary food were the order of the day, with fresh vegetables conspicuous by their absence.

Few would have argued with the premise that when it came to lunchtime menus, schools not only could, but should do better. With sport on the decline, the prevalence of fatty, sugary food was contributing to the health professional's definition of 'a perfect storm'. With a generation of children taking little exercise and eating poorly, those who read the runes were predicting a health time bomb. With obesity on the rise, the prognosis for the future was a rise in heart disease, cancers and diabetes.

Long-term health issues were not the only cause for concern. Any parent who has observed the impact of sweets, cakes and fizzy drinks at a children's party will be aware of the direct relationship between food and behaviour. For teachers dealing with problems ranging from good, old-fashioned rowdiness through to Attention Deficit Disorder, poor quality food was often considered part of the problem.

Underlying all this was a concern that the taste buds of the nation's children were being brutalized by bland, processed meals, spiced up with too much salt and sugar. As such they were being trained to accept a second best option while missing out the experience of nutritious meals prepared with tasty, fresh and healthy ingredients. To a foodie such as Oliver, the desire to educate kids and show them a better way of living and eating was probably as important as concerns about health or educational standards.

But whatever the reasons, by 2005 Oliver had found both a new cause that was worth fighting for – and a vehicle for yet another high-profile TV series.

That series was *Jamie's School Dinners*, which aired on Channel 4 in 2005 and once again set the nation talking. The concept was simple. Oliver would descend on the kitchens of Kidbrooke School in South East London. There he would talk to the dinner ladies, examine the food they were serving and show them how they could do better while sticking to a realistic budget. Later the show would widen out to show how catering could be transformed in schools across the entire London Borough of Greenwich, where Kidbrooke was located.

Part of the appeal was the clash of cultures – the food-obsessed celebrity chef pitted against dinner ladies struggling to serve hundreds of meals a day to hungry kids at a cost per unit of around 36 pence.

On the face of it, at best Oliver's mission could have been seen as naïve and, at worst, patronizing. But it was saved by an underlying agenda that divided both TV viewers and a wider constituency that followed his adventures in the press, on news programmes and TV chat shows. Oliver was seeking not simply to transform school dinners in Kidbrooke School or South East London, he was looking to start a political fire. By shining a torch into the murky secrets of the school canteen, his aim was to shame the government into taking food seriously. He wanted action and *Jamie's School Dinners* was the lever.

There's a parallel with *Jamie's Kitchen* here. Had that show been nothing more than a TV makeover for a handful of trainees then it would have been open to the criticism that it was simply a TV chef adopting a cause for the purposes of reviving a flagging TV career. By leaving a legacy in the shape of the Fifteen Foundation and its restaurants, Oliver answered his critics.

With *Jamie's School Dinners*, Oliver was also determined to leave a legacy but in order to do that he had to get politicians – those with the power to change things – firmly on board.

It should have been a shoe-in. After all, what politician worth his or her salt would fail to rally to the cause of healthier children and better food? The reality was different. The Great British public doesn't always relish being told what to do – even if the instructions are coming from a perky man of the people with an authentic Essex accent. Oliver's attempts to remove chips from menus and introduce real food were met by resistance from both children and parents. As his campaign progressed, there were even press and TV pictures of concerned parents passing parcels of chips and hamburgers through school railings to assuage the appetites of kids traumatized by the sight of fresh vegetables.

Oliver changed the nature of the debate with a mixture of passionate enthusiasm for good food, the facts and figures necessary to swing the argument in his direction and costed solutions that could be put to ministers. Studiedly apolitical, he emerged as a consummate politician

Against this background, political support was hard to come by but Oliver persevered. On and off camera he worked at strategies to encourage children to eat better and developed a range of recipes that would work in the context of the school lunchtime.

Then there was a breakthrough of sorts. Charles Clarke – then the UK Education Secretary – agreed to have an audience with Oliver and it appears there was a meeting of minds. Clarke pledged to find extra cash and the government ultimately agreed to £280m over three years, with £15m of that going to fund the School Food Trust. This was a new organization with a remit to improve nutritional standards by providing schools and local education with research data, information and examples of best practice. The remainder of the cash would go directly to schools and councils. More meetings with politicians followed including an encounter with then Prime Minister Tony Blair.

Oliver was on the political map. He wasn't simply a campaigner, he was a real player.

THE TEAM'S THE THING

Oliver didn't influence government policy on the strength of his charisma alone. Ministers tend to resist initiatives that are stamped with the legend 'not invented here'. Certainly they'll work into the early hours of the morning on their own pet projects or those of their patrons higher up the political pecking order, but they won't always be keen to back ideas dreamed up by pesky members of the general public.

So Oliver had to make a case. During the making of *Jamie's School Dinners*, his researchers at the Fresh One production company were on overdrive, furnishing him with the evidence he needed to demonstrate that lousy food was not only an insult to those who had to eat it, but it was also causing real damage that would have a financial and social cost. Some of the information used by the team was drawn from earlier work on school meals carried out by the Soil Association and campaigner Jeanette Orray.

And Oliver has been careful to welcome any additional government investment while continuing to push for more. Talking about the his campaign on Channel 4's *Jamie's School Dinners* website he stressed that while progress had been made there still a lot to play for. 'Thanks to the massive support we had from the public and the media we were able to get more again this time round. But the reality is that when you work it out at school level, the amounts are tiny.'

Oliver is pushing for some hefty capital spending to improve the standards of school meals. According to the estimates published on the *Jamie's School Dinners* website, £290m is needed to raise standards in schools already equipped with kitchens while a further £350m is required to build catering facilities in establishments that no longer have them.

ACHIEVING AN OUTCOME

Regardless of what the government does next, Oliver has undoubtedly achieved an outcome, both in terms of public spending and parental awareness of nutritional issues. School lunches are healthier – so much so in fact that it is now government policy to encourage pupils to eat in canteens rather than bringing in their own food.

It has to be said that the campaign hasn't been such a hit with the children. In July 2009, the Schools Food Trust published figures showing that just 3m out of 7.9m schoolchildren were eating the new improved, healthy school meals rather than opting for takeaways and packed lunches.

But that shouldn't detract from Oliver's achievements. The issue of school meals was and is a political hot potato. Standards began to fall when school meals services were privatized by the Conservative government in 1989, allowing private contractors to move in with an agenda to cut costs and maximize profits. A freshly elected Labour did little or nothing to improve matters. Indeed, ministerial anxiety to avoid any suggestion that the words New Labour and 'nanny state' were interchangeable, dampened any enthusiasm for prescribing healthy food at the expense of chips and Turkey Twizzlers.

Oliver changed the nature of the debate with a mixture of passionate enthusiasm for good food, the facts and figures necessary to swing the argument in his direction and costed solutions that could be put to ministers. Apparently apolitical, Oliver emerged as the consummate politician.

CAREER BENEFITS

And in the process, he did his own career no harm at all. Neither *Jamie's Kitchen*/Fifteen nor the *Jamie's School Dinners* series were cash cows. He invested his own money in both campaigns and Fifteen in particular was a drain on his resources for several years.

But the benefits to the Oliver brand are immeasurable. Who knows how long the Oliver of *The Naked Chef* fame would have been at the top of the television tree and the best-seller list? TV is always searching for novelty and had the BBC allowed *The Naked Chef* to run its course with several more series, Oliver could well be last year's thing.

But *Jamie's Kitchen* and *Jamie's School Dinners* showed the public a different side of the man – a side they seemed to take to. The result: Oliver continues to sell cookery books, DVDs and his range of branded products in large numbers.

Arguably both series helped open the door to a new breed of food programmes that focused on issues rather than recipes while remaining entertaining to a mass audience. This was a seam that Oliver continued to mine in personal projects such as *Jamie's Fowl Dinners* and *Jamie Saves our Bacon*. Thus, as Oliver continues to develop his career, a mixture of altruism, campaigning zeal and enlightened self-interest have served him very well indeed.

REMEMBER THE SOCIAL DIMENSION

Oliver's persona has come a long way from *The Naked Chef*. His campaigns and socially aware business ventures have achieved some real good in the world while also keeping him well and truly in the public eye. But his initiative to train unemployed teenagers and the School Dinners campaign could have become massively unstuck if they had failed to deliver on their promises. This is how Oliver achieved his goals:

- **Be passionate.** Oliver's campaigns and social initiatives have focused on subjects that he feels engaged with. As a school leaver with just two GCSEs in the A-C band, his commitment to food transformed his life and with *Jamie's Kitchen* he felt it could do the same for disadvantage teenagers. As a father, he was appalled by the quality of school food.
- **Build a good team.** While Oliver's energy and enthusiasm drove the Fifteen and *Jamie's School Dinners* projects, to implement his plans he needed good people around him – be they training professionals, experts in nutrition or the committed researchers of his Fresh One production company.
- **Build something sustainable.** TV series come and go, but in establishing the Fifteen Foundation, Oliver ensured that his vision of a restaurant linked to a training scheme would continue when he moved on to other projects. In the case of the *School Dinners* TV series he remained committed to improving standards long after the series finished.
- **Plan for succession.** As Oliver has withdrawn from day-to-day involvement with Fifteen, his continuing role as a trustee gives him a say in the appointment of key staff who will carry the vision forward.

- **Invest in the vision.** Speaking to Michael Parkinson, Oliver said it was important that he put his own money into Fifteen to ensure that he kept control of the direction of the project and the associated TV programme.
- **Get the facts right.** Lobbying for higher standards in school meals, Oliver ensured that he had facts and costings to back up his calls for more money.

5

BECOME THE FACE OF A SUPERMARKET

With the Christmas of 2004 just around the corner, Clarissa Dickson Wright had little in the way of seasonal good cheer to offer fellow TV chef Jamie Oliver. Although respectful of his cooking, Dickson Wright – one half of BBC2's *Two Fat Ladies* cookery team – seemed outraged by Oliver's appearance in ads promoting Sainsbury's line of farmed salmon. [1]

Citing research claiming that salmon farmed in Europe were contaminated with cancer-causing chemicals, she went on to accuse Oliver of prostituting himself by endorsing a product that he wouldn't eat himself.

This attack on Oliver's integrity reflected a certain unease on the part of many food professionals about his relationship with one of Britain's largest supermarket groups.

Oliver's appeal has helped the company boost sales and enhance its image of a purveyor of quality food and a cool place to shop

Sainsbury's later made comment that all of their fresh salmon is sourced from clean waters, fully compliant with welfare, environmental and safety requirements. A spokesperson for Oliver also reiterated that, 'If it was the sort of thing that he shouldn't have put his name to then he would not have done so.' [2]

Despite the controversy, Oliver's status as the face of Sainsbury's has endured, not least because it has proved enormously beneficial to both parties. To Oliver it has been a welcome source of cash – cash that helped him finance the Fifteen restaurant and School Dinner's projects. Equally important in the dark days between his departure from the BBC and his resurrection on Channel 4, it kept his face on screen.

Sainsbury's has also reaped significant dividends. Oliver's appeal has helped the company boost sales and enhance its image of a purveyor of quality food and a cool place to shop. Without Oliver, it is arguable that Sainsbury's would have struggled in the ongoing battle for sales with rivals Tesco, Asda, Morrisons and Waitrose.

The importance of Oliver's relationship was underlined when the UK began to slip into recession in the wake of the global financial crisis. Not considered the cheapest of supermarkets, Sainsbury's grew sales by 3.9% in the six months to November 2008, stealing market share from its closest competitor Tesco. As the *Financial Times* commented, part of Sainsbury's success could be attributed to yet another campaign featuring Jamie Oliver. This time round the chef was using his ad shots to demonstrate 'How you can feed your family for a fiver'. The concept was simple. In a series of ads Oliver – sometimes accompanied by a gang of equally enthusiastic assistants known as the Try Team – would demonstrate how to cook meals that wouldn't break the bank, and without sacrificing quality.

> **Without Oliver, it is arguable that Sainsbury's would have struggled in the ongoing battle for sales with rivals Tesco, Asda, Morrisons and Waitrose**

Prior to the recession, the Oliver effect was even more pronounced. For instance, in the first quarter of 2006, the supermarket announced a steep hike in like for like sales of 5.3% from a year earlier. At least part of that upsurge was attributable to the company's 'Try something new' campaign. Fronted by Oliver in his 'ambassador for good food' guise, the ads encouraged the Sainsbury's audience to experiment with new ingredients and recipes.

BE YOUR OWN MAN

That campaign demonstrates why the Oliver/Sainsbury's partnership has been so successful. The chef's role in the company's advertising has not been to simply endorse products. The campaigns work best when his passion for food is harnessed to the supermarket's commercial agenda.

For instance, in the 'Feed your family for a fiver' ads he served up quick recipes demonstrating that cutting back on household expenditure doesn't have to involve any sacrifice of taste or nutritional value. It was a message that chimed neatly with his television day job of campaigning on school dinners and home cooking while promoting Sainsbury's as the place to shop. It was a 'win-win'.

Oliver's on-screen relationship with the Sainbury's brand might have panned out very differently. Initially the supermarket group was looking for nothing more than a marketable face and Oliver, at the peak of his early fame with the BBC, fitted the bill.

Reputedly the initial concept was a play on *The Naked Chef* concept and involved Oliver posing unclothed in a bubble bath while encouraging the great British public to shop at Sainsbury's. If he'd gone down that route, his tenure with the supermarket would have followed the tried and trusted formula of cheap and cheerful ads featuring celebrity names as a form of window dressing.

It has to be said that window dressing can be hugely effective. Put a well-known personality on-screen and even something as dull as buying motor insurance or taking out a loan can seem worthwhile watching and a tad more interesting.

It has to be said that window dressing can be hugely effective. Put a well-known personality on screen and even something as dull as buying motor insurance or taking out a loan can seem a tad more interesting

Sometimes the link between the personality and the product can be tenuous to say the least. In recent times, British viewers have been treated to seventies punk rock star Iggy Pop – famous for smearing his semi naked body with peanut butter and diving into the crowd – encouraging us to buy car insurance. Former Sex Pistol Johnny Rotten espoused the delights of a brand of butter. Slightly more believably, film director Michael Winner's name is now indelibly associated with a series of slightly funny/mildly irritating ads for car insurance. Also plugging hard on the car insurance front, upper crust thespians Joanna Lumley and Nigel Havers have been assuring us that you 'you don't have to be posh' to be privileged.

But Oliver wasn't content to be another pretty or well-known face. Whether it was nature, nurture or a mixture of both, he benefitted from industrial strength self-confidence. So when Sainsbury's expressed an interest in using him for a series of ad campaigns, Oliver was willing to put his own ideas on the table at a meeting with the supermarket's then chief executive, Sir Peter Davies. By all accounts Sir Peter was impressed and a deal was done.

Oliver signed on for an initial two years, in a deal that would add just under £1m to his bank account. The chef has always insisted that it wasn't just about the money. As he has consistently told reporters, his intention was to encourage his new found paymaster to improve the quality of food sold in its stores.

That was a long-term goal. In the shorter term, Oliver ensured that the ads were as much about the preparation of food as they were about Sainsbury's. Much to the discomfort of the BBC, he was doing much the same in a 30 or 60 second ad slot as he had been doing on *The Naked Chef* – gathering together with friends and showing them how to cook. In that respect he remained true to his own brand values while simultaneously promoting the brand of a third party.

The ads are informative as well as carrying a commercial message

It was a class act and a hugely successful one. Oliver's natural peer group were young men of his own age – single (or at least unencumbered by children), relatively affluent and not particularly inclined towards cooking, unless you count heating a ready meal as cooking. Oliver used this market as his on-screen audience while he demonstrated how to knock up, say, prawn curry from ingredients that happened to be available from your local Sainsbury's. It's debatable whether Oliver's efforts on *The Naked Chef* or his Sainsbury's ads encouraged significantly more of his peers to cook, but one thing was certain: when Oliver's first series of ads were broadcast, sales of the ingredients he used soared. He may not have been reaching the young males of the *Loaded*-reading generation, but the surge in demand for nutmeg, vanilla pods and herbs showed that he was certainly reaching someone.

Oliver also wanted the supermarket to diversify and in that respect he also had some success. For instance he persuaded his paymaster to increase the range of herbs on offer, thus introducing the exotic delights of lemon thyme, lemon basil and purple thyme to Sainsbury's shoppers.

Affirmation that the Oliver effect was doing the business came in the swift renewal of the young man's contract. In 2002 he was offered a reputed £2m to sign on for another year and since then he has played an important role in the company's overall marketing mix.

BE ADAPTABLE BUT STAY ON MESSAGE

And as the years have gone by his ads have changed in line with the requirements of the supermarket. We've seen Oliver at Christmas, dressed as a Victorian gentleman dispensing seasonal tips on how to spice up our party food. And we've seen Jamie admonishing us for filling our baskets with the same thing and encouraging us to 'try something new'. Later he promoted the same message with 'girls' from the Sainsbury's Try Team as they ventured out around the shopping centres and public spaces of Britain urging us to be more adventurous. As the recession closed in, Oliver and the Try Team turned their attention to money-saving solutions with the 'Feed the family for a fiver' campaign.

We've also seen Oliver's own celebrity firepower augmented and enhanced by that of others. Christmas 2008 saw the chef 'accidentally' bumping into the ITV Saturday night ratings favourites Ant and Dec. True to stereotype the duo were buying canned pineapple chunks for their party. Needless to say, Oliver was quick to invite them home to demonstrate a more imaginative menu.

But the message has always been the same. As Bobby Hui, advertising director at advertising agency Saatchi and Saatchi told *Retail Week* magazine in a review of the supermarket's 2007 Christmas ads: 'Sainsbury's has not veered from its strategy, which is all about using Jamie as a vehicle to help you make the most of your food. It has great suggestions for the party season and Oliver has great delivery. He still appears to be very much the man of the moment.'³

MAKE YOURSELF INDISPENSIBLE

It would be naïve to suggest that Oliver has singlehandedly enabled Sainsbury's to fight an increasingly successful battle for market share against its rival supermarket chains.

Even with Oliver's ads already proving popular, the supermarket group went through a bad time in the early 2000s, while Tesco – its nearest competitor in terms of public perception of price and quality – went from strength to strength.

The turnaround came with the appointment of new CEO, Justin King, in 2004. A 'new broom', he implemented a campaign of cost cutting while also replacing an automated system that had been causing problems, ensuring that stores were properly stocked up.

Working with ad agency Abbot Mead Vickers BBDO and Oliver, he changed the perception of the company – certainly in terms of its value-for-money proposition – by implementing the 'Feed your family for a fiver' campaign. By 2009, a company that had been widely seen as a food industry also-ran by market analysts was bucking the recessionary trend by planning 50 new stores.

But Oliver has played a hugely important part in the company's transformation. Perhaps he isn't quite indispensible – after all, who is? But without him the supermarket would have lost a face that has become inextricably associated with its own brand.

RETAIN YOUR INDEPENDENCE

Oliver and Sainsbury's may be cosily tucked up in bed together but they aren't joined at the hip. Indeed, one of the characteristics of the relationship is that each party – in public at least – has been tolerant of the other straying 'off message'.

Take the simple question of where Oliver does his own shopping. Shortly after taking the Sainsbury's shilling he announced publicly that he didn't shop there. Probably not the most sensitive public comment to make but just to rub it in, he added. 'I buy from specialist growers, organic suppliers and farmers. It is completely about non-compromise', he told *The Independent* in 2001.[4]

Was this a gaff? Was it naïvety on the part of the young star? Was it refreshing honesty or a need to assert independence? Whatever the reasons behind his comments, the critics leapt in with accusations of hypocrisy. How could he extol the virtues of the grocery chain and then barefacedly admit to going elsewhere for asparagus, runner beans and herbs?

The quote was less than sensitive. Few of us really expect celebrities to exclusively consume the products they endorse, but most refrain from making public statements that appear to undermine the marketing activity they've taken part in and been amply paid for.

But Oliver was being specific. His comments referred to his status as consultant chef at Monte's, not his own shopping habits. In that context it's not surprising that he preferred to go direct to growers rather than popping down to the nearest supermarket.

Content to let the storm blow itself out was the line that Sainsbury's took. 'We have an excellent relationship with Jamie, and we don't usually supply restaurants', said another spokesman. 'So there's nothing unusual going on', Sainsbury's said in a statement.[5]

By the same token, Sainsbury's has not always seemed to support its man and his business ventures. For instance, when Oliver launched a new range of herbs and pasta sauces in 2008, Tesco happily placed orders while Sainsbury's dragged its feet. Indeed, according to a report in the *Daily Telegraph*, the supermarket agreed to stock just a few jars and items from the 40-strong portfolio of products. The newspaper also managed to dig out a non-attributed spokesperson who stressed that it was a decision made for sound business reasons. He emphasized that they look at the differences between new and existing ranges to determine whether a new product will be added. In some cases, as in this one, the differences were not as apparent so the decision was made not to take the products on. The spokesperson stressed however: 'This is in no way a snub to Jamie.'[6]

Both incidents must have proved galling to some within the Oliver and Sainsbury's camps but it's not hard to see an upside. When Oliver announced that he didn't buy his restaurant products from Sainsbury's – or indeed any supermarket – he was laying down a marker on his own integrity and independence. That integrity was an important part of his appeal that has been used successfully by the Sainsbury's group.

Equally Sainsbury's reported reluctance to swallow the Oliver product range hook, line, and sinker could have been a blessing in disguise for the young man, perhaps making it easier to sell the range to rival chains. Mirroring Sainsbury's relaxed approach to Oliver's declaration that he didn't buy from them for his restaurant, a spokesman tabled an equally sanguine response: 'These are lovely products that Jamie hopes will be in as many retailers as possible. Tesco just happens to be the first to make a decision to stock them.'[7]

The message? Both parties are free to make their own business decisions.

RIDE OUT THE STORM

Less easy to brush over was Oliver's reaction to a failure by Sainsbury's to attend a TV show on the welfare of chickens. Like fellow chef Hugh Fearnley-Whittingstall, Oliver is an enthusiastic meat eater but both men are also passionate about maintaining high standards of farm animal welfare. Their TV battleground on this issue was the treatment of the chickens and hens that provide our eggs and healthy white meat.

The practices of the poultry industry have been under scrutiny for years. The treatment of chickens has been largely a story of coffin-like cramped conditions in huge sheds where the animals never see the light of day from birth to death. In separate programmes for Channel 4, Oliver and Fearnley-Whittingstall set out to highlight this in order to change public opinion about buying intensively farmed chicken. By demonstrating just how wretched the conditions were, they hoped a) to encourage consumers to buy only humanely and responsibly produced poultry and b) for supermarkets to deploy welfare benchmarks such as the RSPCA's Freedom Foods standard.

Oliver's contribution to the debate was a programme entitled *Jamie's Fowl Dinners* in which he – among other things – gassed a chicken on screen and in front of a live audience. Sainsbury's had been invited to attend but did not send a representative. An angry Oliver responded by saying: 'I am really upset. The question is why they didn't come. What is there to hide? It is shocking that the people I work for didn't turn up on the day. I don't know why.'

In fairness to Sainsbury's, Tesco, Asda and Morrisons also failed to show up for the live debate. You could well ask why would they? Supermarkets face the task of balancing their animal welfare policies with providing food that their customers can afford. Almost by definition, 'affordable' eggs and chicken meat are going to be reared more intensively than their free-range counterparts. While that in itself is no secret, few supermarket PR people would relish entering a live debate where their buying policies are taken to task. Animal welfare is a sensitive issue for supermarkets.

In its own defence, Sainsbury's also pointed out that it had agreed to an interview with a spokesman to be shown as part of the show. But Oliver's public disappointment was not something that could easily be brushed off. Sainsbury's had been publicly called to account by one of its most important public endorsees.

In the event, Oliver appeared to avoid a confrontation. After discussions with Sainsbury's and its CEO Justin King he issued a statement that couldn't have been more fulsome in its praise for the company. 'I am happy to confirm what I have said on several occasions: that Sainsbury's has the most to be proud of on this important animal welfare issue. Indeed I would not have continued working with Sainsbury's for so many years if I did not believe that you were showing real leadership. Your team have been particularly helpful.'[8]

Needless to day, Sainsbury's was equally fulsome in return, with CEO King going out of his way to heap praise on his star turn. 'We're very happy with Jamie. I mean, he's someone who's got an independence of mind and that independence of mind is actually a great benefit to Sainsbury's.'[8] It was another bullet dodged. The relationship survived and continues to thrive – despite the bumps and bangs.

Which brings us neatly back to the comments of Clarissa Dickson Wright. Behind the colourful language, she raised a serious question – is it possible for a figure who is trusted by the public to be so closely associated with a commercial organization and what happens when the views of the individual fall out of step with those of the employer?

> ... when push comes to shove his status as a face of Sainsbury's hasn't deterred him from championing some controversial causes in his TV career

In fact, Oliver has more or less successfully managed to walk the tightrope. His ads for Sainsbury's are well thought of within the industry and popular with the public, and produce the required dividends for Sainsbury's too.

And for the most part, Oliver has retained his integrity. The ads are informative as well as carrying a commercial message and when push comes to shove his status as the face of Sainsbury's hasn't deterred him from championing controversial causes in his TV career. He has also been careful to avoid endorsing products that wouldn't comply with his own values. 'I don't advertise junk food for Sainsbury's. Everything I advertise for them is scrupulously policed', he told *The Independent*.[9]

He's also more than prepared to defend the ads he has made, including the one featuring farmed salmon that so incensed Clarissa Dickson Wright. 'The tidal loch the salmon comes from was the best of its kind. British people need to eat more fish', he said in the same interview.

That's also a plus point for Sainsbury's. Oliver the passionate campaigner for better nutrition and appreciation of food makes a powerful advocate for the supermarket.

There are, however, limits. As the *Fowl Dinners* affair demonstrated, biting the hand that feeds – even with righteous intent – is not always wise. Oliver's statement in praise of Sainsbury's animal welfare record may well have been heartfelt but in the court of public opinion it, perhaps in the minds of some, dented his credibility. Not enough so as to inflict severe damage, but certainly sufficient to give the ever circling critics something to chew on.

The success of the Sainsbury's campaigns has been due in no small part to the clever splicing of Oliver's own brand values with those of the supermarket. It's a good trick if you can pull it off, but it remains a tightrope act.

BECOME THE FACE OF A SUPERMARKET

Jamie Oliver has established an ongoing relationship with the Sainsbury's supermarket chain. It's a relationship that has allowed him to be true to his own television persona while successfully promoting the company's products. To some extent he has also succeeded in encouraging Sainsbury's to carry a more diverse range of foods. But the close relationship between his mainstream television work and the ads he fronts for Sainsbury's has made it a tricky relationship to handle. In particular it is debatable whether his role in promoting the commercial agenda of a business is compatible with his role as a food campaigner. Here's how he has managed to square the circle.

- **Negotiate the terms of the deal.** Oliver had turned down other offers before joining forces with Sainsbury's. Before signing up for the first year, he met with the supermarket's then CEO, Sir Peter Davies and made it clear he wanted his own ideas incorporated into the campaign.
- **Retain your own brand values.** Oliver's ads for Sainsbury's not only tapped into the persona he had already developed for *The Naked Chef* but also the spirit of the popular BBC show. In particular he surrounded himself with friends, relatives and sometimes show business peers, dispensing tips on cooking using Sainsbury's ingredients.
- **Keep your paymaster at arms length.** This is a tricky one. Oliver has occasionally made off message statements that jar with his role as a figure associated with Sainsbury's. Most famously he declared that he didn't shop there for his restaurant. The statement emphasized the distinction between Oliver the restaurateur and Oliver the supermarket

figurehead but it had the potential to put stress on a relationship that was otherwise working well.

- **Know when to be diplomatic.** More serious was Oliver's public disappointment over Sainsbury's failure to participate in a live debate on the welfare of chickens. Following private discussions between Sainsbury's and Oliver, the latter issued a statement praising the supermarket's stance on animal welfare issues.

- **Keep it fresh.** Working with Sainsbury's and advertising agency Abbot Mean Vickers BBDO, Oliver has succeeded in keeping the ads fresh in the face of a changing commercial agenda. For instance, as Sainsbury's cut costs and emphasized value, Oliver fronted the 'Feed your family for a fiver' campaign. The ads chimed with themes Oliver was promoting in his television work – healthy food on a budget – while repositioning Sainsbury's as a good value place to shop.

- **Know your value.** After the initial success of the ads, Oliver was able to secure a better cash deal. The money came in handy when he needed to fund the Fifteen restaurant experiment.

6

DEAL WITH ADVERSITY

''ve got to hand it to you little brother – you certainly know how to pick yourself up after a tumble.'

That was fictional oil baron, JR Ewing paying a rare compliment to his ethically minded brother Bobby after the younger sibling had extricated himself from one of those tightly plotted traps that characterized 70s soap opera *Dallas*. The reliably unscrupulous JR was right to be impressed. The ability to deal with adversity and snatch victory from the jaws of defeat in a crisis tends to be underrated in the business world. Business leaders talk about their successes

The world is full of individuals who are more than capable of prospering when times are good. As a wise man once said, a monkey with a banana stall could make money in a rising market. But arguably the real test of a business leader is his or her ability to cope with the setbacks and sudden shocks that commercial life invariably throws up. Indeed, those who don't have the wisdom, skill, strength of character and often sheer good luck to cope with difficult situations are often the first to join the casualty list when the commercial tide begins to turn.

Jamie Oliver is not a businessman in the mould of, say, a Jack Welch, an Alan Sugar or even a Richard Branson. He is, first and foremost, a television presenter, chef and food campaigner who has gone on to build a diversified business around the strength of his personality and a very recognizable set of brand values.

In some respects he's in an enviable position. Income from TV and books hedges the risk of making a loss from his growing range of business ventures. Equally, as his businesses take on a commercial life that is independent from his media work then, if his star wanes, there will always be something to fall back on.

But he's also in jeopardy. Commercial life throws up its own problems that we read about every day in the business press. Companies fail because of recession, bad cash flow management, changing markets and bad decision making. Badly run companies go under, while the good ones ride out the storm. A growing business empire means that Oliver will have to face up to a whole range of challenges as he rolls out restaurants and introduces new products onto the shelves. At the same time, experience has taught him that the world of media contains no shortage of its own hidden trapdoors.

Saying the wrong thing. Doing the wrong thing. Boring the public. All of these sins can wreck careers in double quick time

In the recent past, we've seen apparently unassailable television stars paying for errors made on the air. Comedian Russell Brand stood down from his BBC presenter role after leaving inappropriate messages on the answerphone of a non-showing guest. Partner in crime Jonathan Ross kept his BBC job but was suspended without pay for several months.

Others are not so lucky. The recent death of one-time king of Saturday TV, Simon Dee, was a reminder that even enormously popular presenters can lose everything overnight. In the 1960s, Dee's teatime show attracted audiences that today's presenters and producers would cheerfully kill for. His downfall came when he alienated his employer, the BBC, by campaigning in support of pirate radio while also attacking the then Labour government. Banished from the airways he spent the next four decades in obscurity. Controversy has so far worked for Jamie Oliver, but it proved the end of the road for Dee.

Conventional businessmen can also fall victim to public lapses of judgement. Witness the tragedy that befell Gerald Ratner – one time boss of the Ratners jewellery chain. A fixture on most UK high streets, Ratners was a fantastically successful business. All that changed when Gerald Ratner gave a speech to the Institute of Directors that appeared to both criticize his company's products and, by extension, insult his customers.

Addressing his fellow directors, Ratner joked that a prawn sandwich would last longer than earrings bought from his store and later described a sherry decanter (also sold in his shops) as 'crap'. His remarks were picked up by the media and in the furore that followed, the jewellery chain's sales collapsed. Ratner was forced off the board. The chain was rebranded as Signet but by then the damage had already been done.

The moral of these stories is that those in the public eye are, by their very nature, personalities who trade – at least to some extent – on their ability to communicate, inspire and provoke thought. All well and good, but big, larger-than-life personalities can make big errors of judgment. The business leader who is famed for his wit, candour, or analytical skills will always be in demand whenever journalists need a quote or the local Chamber of Commerce requires a speaker. After all, everyone loves a good, honest commentator. But if an unguarded comment that delights friends or an audience of business peers also alienates the customer or the employer, the result can be a career nosedive.

Jamie Oliver has survived and thrived in the public arena but he came very close to cutting his career short when the BBC – thwarted by the star's refusal to end his relationship with the supermarket chain – decided not to recommission *The Naked Chef* TV show. A period in the wilderness followed as Oliver tried to negotiate deals with other broadcasters. Since then, he has learned not simply to cope with adversity but to use it to his advantage.

HOW TO LOSE FRIENDS AND ALIENATE PEOPLE

The BBC's relationship with Oliver began to cool when the young star signed up make a series of adverts for the Sainsbury's supermarket group. Ostensibly there was nothing wrong with that. TV personalities – be they actors or presenters – frequently cross over to 'the dark side' of the advertising world. Ad agencies are always in search of well-known faces that the public like and trust. Likewise, high-profile people are seldom averse to making a few extra pounds by providing voiceovers or endorsing products on screen.

But the BBC decided that Oliver's relationship with Sainsbury's was a little too close to the BBC bone. For one thing, the nature of the supermarket's campaign blurred the boundaries between Oliver as a programme maker and Oliver as an asset whose role was to drive Sainsbury's sales.

The deal with Sainsbury's didn't have an immediate effect on his TV career, although there were misgivings at the BBC over the style of the early ads. His work for the supermarket was too close to what he was doing on *The Naked Chef*. In both situations, he was surrounded by friends and family showing how simple ingredients could be used to create delicious food.

In fairness, Oliver approached the Sainsbury's work with integrity. Insisting on being much more than a puppet, he fed ideas back into the Supermarket's boardroom, encouraging the company to improve the range of ingredients available for a new generation of enthusiastic foodies. In a neat feedback loop, the ideas generated by Oliver – notably a much wider choice of herbs – became a selling point for the supermarket. As Oliver said: 'Working with Sainsbury's gives me the chance to reach and inspire millions of customers with fresh new ideas on making the most of Sainsbury's top quality foods and ingredients.'[1]

Arguably Oliver's integrity made matters worse. Had he been content to be little more than a pretty face endorsing the Sainsbury's brand, then the BBC might not have been quite so concerned. But the commitment to good quality produce he displayed in his work for Sainsbury's mirrored the stance he took on *The Naked Chef*. There was bound to be some conflict of interest.

But although we viewers know that celebrity is all about smoke and mirrors – perception rather than reality – we don't always like it when the curtain is pulled back, allowing us to see the reality behind

The crunch came when Oliver featured in an ad campaign for Sainsbury's Blue Parrot range of meals. The ads were run while the third series of *The Naked Chef* was still on TV, allegedly breaking a back room agreement between the corporation and the supermarket chain. The scheduling of the ads for the supermarket giant's Blue Parrot Café range of children's meals meant that they clashed with repeats of Oliver's cookery series screened on BBC2, causing viewers to potentially become confused according to the BBC.[2] Consequently, the corporation declined to commission a fourth series of *The Naked Chef* leaving Oliver without a televisual home.

'I got sacked', Oliver told TV producer Peter Bazalgette in a face-to-face interview at the Edinburgh television festival in 2008. 'I kind of did. They felt that the Sainsbury's ads looked like *The Naked Chef*. I wanted to stay but they wanted me to personally indemnify the programme.'[3]

PICK YOURSELF UP AND DUST YOURSELF DOWN

In theory it shouldn't have been a problem for the rising star. He was still one of the most popular television presenters in the country and even without a fourth BBC series in the pipeline, he could reasonably expect a rival broadcaster to take him on board. Meanwhile, he had the Sainsbury's ads to keep his face in the public eye.

And in some respects it was a chance to move on. *The Naked Chef* had been made by independent TV production company Optomen for the BBC. When the corporation didn't green light a fourth series, he took the opportunity to set up his own production company, Fresh One. For Optomen that was doubtless a cruel blow, but for Oliver it was an opportunity to take full control of the exploitation of his television persona. He had put a marker in the ground, declaring that he was very much his own man.

But the road ahead would be far from easy. For an edgy personality with youth appeal, Oliver should have been a natural for Channel 4. Truth to tell, though, Oliver may have changed the language and grammar of the TV cookery show but behind the 'cool' London flat, the trendy on-screen friends and the star's trademark Essex vernacular lay a traditional recipe show that appealed to a middle-class audience in search of a breath of fresh air. In many ways his natural home was BBC2.

Certainly Channel 4 seemed in no hurry to commission an Oliver series and while his tenure as consultant chef at Monte's Restaurant in Knightsbridge coupled with his work for Sainsbury's meant that he would never be short of cash, he acted quickly to retain a channel of communication to his wider public.

In 2000, ahead of his split with the BBC, Oliver had already produced *Pukka Tukka*, a DVD of material that that hadn't been shown on TV.

But in the period following his BBC bust-up it was live appearances that provided the means for Oliver to cement his relationship with the public. This was achieved through the Oliver's tour of live *Happy Days* shows, produced in associated with the International Management Group.

First rolled out on the stage of Hammersmith Apollo, *Happy Days* was an indicator of Oliver's potential as an entertainment 'draw'. The concept was simple. Oliver performs in front of a live crowd. He was freed from the constraints of the TV studio and in this environment he could extend the informal social feel of his TV shows by bringing members of the audience on stage to help him. In addition, wife Jools was there to help him via a giant video screen and staff from Monte's restaurant were on hand too. In Oliver's own words, it was 'the best tasting live cooking show ever'. [4] After Hammersmith the show went on to tour the UK, Australia and New Zealand.

But if Oliver was keeping busy, there was arguably a real need to get back on UK TV. Live shows only work if the star at the centre of the event has the pulling power to put 3000 bums on seats for a single show. Oliver's draw was undoubtedly in this ballpark, but his celebrity wouldn't necessarily last unless it was regularly refreshed by appearances on television.

REINVENT AND MOVE FORWARD

Ultimately Oliver returned to his natural home by reinventing himself. In the months that had followed his arrival in London, the yet-to-be discovered chef was chatting with a friend who worked with problem kids. The eureka moment came when she described how these aggressive and troubled teenagers were often calmed by the process of making food together.

The anecdote stuck with Oliver and during his career hiatus between the BBC and Channel 4 he developed a plan that would have an on-screen and off-screen life. In the 'real' world he established a restaurant – Fifteen – which provided training to unemployed teenagers. On-screen, the cameras would follow the efforts of Oliver and his colleagues from the catering industry as they attempted to mould sometimes difficult kids into trained professionals. The series – *Jamie's Kitchen* – would be a long way removed from the happy lifestyle presented by *The Naked Chef*. It certainly had food at its core, but the appeal lay in witnessing the real life drama that was a disparate mix of previously non-achieving teenagers struggling to turn their lives around. Oliver was at the centre of that drama – often stressed and apparently struggling to make the right decisions. The camera followed him at work and at home, revealing the stresses within the Oliver marriage as family life and the demands of the project fought for his time.

Arguably the Oliver brand at this point was in need of reinvention. He had always divided opinion, polarizing the viewing public into those who loved his untutored charm and those who loathed the Essex accent and his Jack-the-Lad approach to life and cooking. As his fame grew, so did the critical sniping.

Witness journalist Jan Moir's comments in the *Daily Telegraph* back in 2001. Assigned to interview the young chef in his role as consultant at Monte's private members club, she made her position clear.

When confronted with the suggestion that a significant proportion of the UK population found him annoying rather than inspiring, Oliver was bullish. 'So they don't like me? So what. At the end of the day, they can always switch over or not buy the book.'[5]

As is turned out the interview reads like something of a hatchet job. When Oliver met with Moir in the restaurant, he was wearing chef's apparel and sought to give the impression that he'd been playing a hands-on role in the kitchens prior to the interview. Moir accused him of doing no such thing. The journalist reckoned he had donned the white jacket and apron immediately before the meeting.

There was worse to come. As the interview progressed, Moir questioned the authenticity of the persona Oliver had created. To his fans he was the real deal. A young man who combined communications skills and a way with people that allowed him to mix with market traders and royalty alike. Above all, he was a nice guy. Moir thought she detected someone who was much more calculating.

One could argue that Jan Moir was being more than a little hard on Oliver. While the public might like to think he was little changed from the chirpy kitchen worker who was plucked to stardom from obscurity, the reality was that Oliver was now a firmly established part of the celebrity firmament. Why then shouldn't he have his hair styled courtesy of Charles Worthington? Why shouldn't he promote his brand? After all, television was a career not a hobby.

If Oliver had donned a chef's outfit minutes before shaking hands with Moir, Oliver was doing nothing more than playing to the gallery. It was a bit of theatrics to enhance his image. But Moir's article worried that in promoting 'brand Oliver', the chef might be in danger of tarnishing it. And whilst we viewers know that celebrity is a lot about smoke and mirrors – perception rather than reality – we don't always like it when the curtain is pulled back.

Witness the furore over celebrity chef Gordon Ramsay when it was revealed that a fish he had apparently harpooned on a TV cookery show had actually been speared by someone else. On TV, Ramsay had emerged triumphant from the ocean, brandishing his prize. In reality, a spearfishing expert was sent out beforehand to ensure Ramsay had something to cook.[6] Then there was the case of TV grandee Alan Yentob. As frontman of arts programme *Imagine*, he apparently interviewed a series of high profile subjects, in person and face-to-face. In a number of cases someone else had done the interview and Yentob's questions and reactions were later edited-in ahead of the footage being broadcast.[7]

Jamie's Kitchen **and** *Jamie's School Dinners* **have probably ensured that Oliver will remain on our screens for many years to come**

Moir's account questioned whether Oliver was everything he seemed or claimed to be. The authentic man of the people had a manufactured side. And Moir's remarks about the star's hair stylist and his celebrity lifestyle added to the impression that 'our Jamie', the Essex-born man of the people, was somehow slipping away to be replaced by just another TV celeb on the make.

Press criticism of Oliver was on the rise as his relationship with the BBC cooled and the row over the Sainsbury's ads added more grist to the critics' mill. In the time-honoured tradition of 'building them up then knocking them down', the UK press went to town, attacking everything from his Essex vowel sounds to his Sainsbury's ads and the stylistic excesses of his shows.

DEALING WITH ADVERSITY ON SCREEN

In some respects, Oliver's re-emergence as the socially concerned Oliver of *Jamie's Kitchen* was a masterstroke of reinvention. Leaving aside the clear commitment to what he was doing, in sheer business terms the Channel 4 series breathed new life into a brand that had been flagging.

Here was an Oliver who was much as we remembered him, only perhaps deeper, more vulnerable and likeable. The vocabulary, vowel sounds and irrepressible character were still in place, but added to the mix we had the vision, commitment, stubbornness and sheer good will to undertake such an ambitious project with difficult kids.

In clawing his way back to our TV sets, Oliver demonstrated his ability to ride out storms and bounce back after a setback. In *Jamie's Kitchen* and future series such as *Jamie's School Dinners* he would lay those attributes in front of the public.

In both series, what the public saw was Oliver learning to manage major projects in full view of the camera with no guarantee of success. For instance in *Jamie's School Dinners* he was faced not only with the task of serving healthy food in 55 schools at a budget of 36 pence per plate, but also overcoming the resistance of pupils raised on chips and Turkey Twizzlers, not to mention the scepticism of dinner ladies with no particular inclination to change the status quo. In *Jamie's Kitchen* much of the on-screen drama centred on people management, with Oliver learning to deal with the emotional traumas of working with a diverse group of young people. Knowing when to be tough and when to show a more sympathetic side was one of the major learning curves depicted on screen.

> **... his re-emergence as the socially concerned Oliver of *Jamie's Kitchen* was a masterstroke of reinvention**

STAYING ON TOP

Jamie's Kitchen and *Jamie's School Dinners* have probably ensured that Oliver will remain on our screens for many years to come. Since they were first broadcast (in 2005 and 2007 respectively), the reinvigorated Oliver has continued to keep his persona fresh. The campaigner is still very much in evidence, in series that have followed his attempts to improve the diet of Rotherham, Yorkshire and raise awareness about animal welfare standards. Meanwhile, he has established himself as a trusty travelling companion in road trips around Italy and the US in search of characters and culinary delights. We see him at home again too. Substituting the London pad for the rural idyll, *Jamie at Home* finds him imparting culinary wisdom from a suitably aspirational home, complete with vegetable garden, chickens and pizza ovens.

Oliver's run-in with the BBC could have been a serious setback for a career that had barely begun. The fact that he returned triumphantly to the screen illustrates a willingness and ability to reinvent his brand, take risks with his talent and come up with ideas that produce compelling television.

DEAL WITH ADVERSITY

Jamie Oliver has always attracted his fair share of criticism and controversy, most of which has served to enhance rather than detract from the strength of his personal brand. In the early stages of his career a decision to appear in ads for the Sainsbury's supermarket group while also working for the BBC threatened his career. However, he returned to TV stronger than before. This is how he did it.

- **Keep your name in front of the public.** Even with no TV shows in the offing, Oliver was still a popular figure. That meant he was still selling books and DVDs. He also took to the live circuit, hosting the *Happy Days* live show in theatres across the UK and abroad.
- **Come up with good ideas.** With the BBC out of the picture, other broadcasters were notably slow to snap Oliver up. The breakthrough came with documentary/reality-style TV programmes *Jamie's Kitchen* and *Jamie's School Dinners*, very different shows from that of *The Naked Chef*.

- **Reinvent the image.** The Oliver brand was beginning to look tired. Critics were questioning Oliver's authenticity and the cheeky Essex chap persona was beginning to wear thin. *Jamie's Kitchen* provided an opportunity to show a much more complex character on screen.
- **Move forward and diversify.** Since then, Oliver has introduced a considerable degree of variety into his shows, which range from lifestyle/recipe formats to culinary travelogues and campaigning documentaries.
- **Take control.** By forming his own production company, Oliver has seized the freedom to develop his own brand and generate ideas for shows. The same company has also diversified into producing shows for other presenters and personalities.

7

GO INTERNATIONAL

Thanks to the profit-hungry efforts of BBC Worldwide, the young Jamie Oliver became an international star almost as rapidly as he charmed audiences in the UK. Once the first series of *The Naked Chef* was in the can, the commercial arm of the BBC ensured that it was sold and seen around the world. At its peak, it was seen in more than fifty countries.

Oliver's output after leaving the BBC was less universal in character. From *Jamie's Kitchen* through *Jamie's School Dinners* to *Jamie's Ministry of Food*, Oliver's reality TV shows have been focused on very British subject matter. And yet his international popularity appears to be unaffected. His new shows have also proved a cash cow for Channel 4 and his own Fresh One production company and though the numbers rise and fall, recent estimates suggest his programmes are shown in more than 100 countries.

That international success is underlined by recent figures from his holding company, which announced a profit of £7m in 2008 compared with £3.7m the previous year. Talking to *The Guardian* newspaper, a spokesman for the company said the rise in profits was to a large extent attributable to rising overseas sales of his books and programmes, a trend that helped to offset the start-up losses incurred by Oliver's expanding chain of UK-based Italian restaurants. [1]

But Oliver is more than a 'pop-star' chef with an international profile. As in the UK, abroad he has used his celebrity to open up new avenues for his non-media businesses. Alongside the syndicated TV shows that can be seen across five continents, he has also been opening restaurants internationally. In a new development, he has also signed up to produce a series of six shows, specifically for the US market. Oliver is well along the road to becoming a global brand.

JOIN THE BRITISH INVASION

Oliver is probably the closest thing the current world of cooking has to a pop star. So it should probably be no surprise at all that he has successfully conquered the world market. Britain is very good at exporting pop culture and when *The Naked Chef* hit the screens, Oliver clearly had a face that could be exploited. His youthful appeal was very much in keeping with the spirit of the Britpop and 'cool Britannia' exports.

In the guise of the Naked Chef he succeeded in capturing hearts and minds in television markets that are not always easy ground for British shows. It was perhaps unsurprising that his youthful, informal style secured big audiences on Australia's Channel 2, but he also became a popular fixture on the USA's Food Network and France's Gourmand Channel. His cross channel success was, of course, particularly sweet for those with an Anglo Saxon axe to grind. As the stereotype has it, cooking is a religion in France, and yet here was a bumptious boy from Essex showing the locals how it was done.

At this point, it's worth remembering that Oliver was by no means the only Brit on the international stage. The BBC had a package of programmes to sell into international markets and the dawning era of subject-specific channels on multi-channel cable and satellite services had created a lot of airtime that had to be filled. So when Oliver's programmes were aired in the US, American viewers were also enjoying a menu of British chefs that included the Two Fat Ladies and Ainsley Harriott.

It was Oliver, however, that made the biggest impact.

His early international success was fuelled by the famous motor-mouth. During his interview with Jan Moir, he commented that his was the first cookery programme to be sold to France Italy and Spain, and was in 34 countries over 60 channels.[2]

And there was a certain amount of truth in that. Prior to Oliver, Cool Britannia had been pretty good at turning out pop stars, musicians, actors, directors and designers of international renown. Culturally, a post-Beatles 'brand UK' had always punched above its weight in the international market place. British food, however, tended be something of an international joke – even in America, the land of the burger. As Oliver helpfully added, 'They think that we eat slop, that our produce is crap, all our meat is f***ed and that it rains all the time.'[3]

Britain is very good at exporting pop culture ...

But international perceptions of UK cuisine had been changing. As the foodie boom of the 1980s and 1990s unfolded, tourists coming to the UK discovered that the great British diet did not entirely consist of pie and chips. Throughout the country – but particularly in London and the Home Counties – there were good restaurants serving a wide range of cuisines. True, despite the good efforts of the Two Fat Ladies to celebrate traditional English and British cooking, the UK didn't have a particularly good reputation for its indigenous cuisine. But in the grand tradition of Britain's empire builders scouring the world and bringing everything they found back home, UK chefs were very good at taking the best from other people's cooking traditions and, where necessary, transforming them for the British palate. In Oliver's case his biggest inspiration was Italy.

But even if Oliver can't lay claim to singlehandedly leading a revival in international interest in British cooking, we can't really begrudge him his claim as 'ambassador'. As in the UK, international audiences warmed to his enthusiasm, energy and ability to sweep away the snobbery and mystique associated with high-grade cooking. And in doing so he demonstrated that the Brits were just as capable as their US, Australian, French or German counterparts.

... when *The Naked Chef* **hit the screens Oliver clearly had a face that could be exploited. His youthful appeal was very much in keeping with the spirit of Britpop and cool Britannia**

And Oliver put the same effort into promoting his brand internationally. In the US alone, he's swapped comic lines with the likes of chat show hosts David Letterman and Jay Leno and swapped cookery tips with national treasure Oprah Winfrey. He's even shared a screen (and a grill pan) with Tom Cruise. The US chat show circuit is a pretty demanding beast. On this side of the Atlantic, appear on Jonathan Ross or Graham Norton and your hosts will get the laughs on your behalf (and sometimes at your expense). On the US circuit you're expected to go out and entertain. Although he can sometimes appear strangely restrained when outside of his own TV comfort zone – the recipe show and the drama doc – Oliver proved he could hold his own in the face of a hyped-up audience, impatient for the next one liner. Indeed, he generally seemed perfectly at home amid the glitz of the US entertainment industry. That translated into higher viewing figures and more books sold.

But there are other benefits too. With an international profile, Oliver also has a market for the range of products that are sold under his name. These days, you'll find his kitchenware and his magazines on the shelves of overseas stores. The US in particular has an appetite for goods touched with Oliver's particular brand of stardust.

THE FRANCHISE GAME

Aside from developing a TV-based brand, Oliver didn't emerge as a businessman proper until he hit on the idea of setting up the Fifteen restaurant. It was a social enterprise in which all profits would be recycled into training, but if the concept was to work, Fifteen had to operate on commercial lines. In other words, it had to attract and retain customers if it was to earn the cash to fulfil its mission. The Fifteen that featured in the *Jamie's Kitchen* TV series was established in 2002 and located just off City Road in East London. But its success led to the experiment being duplicated elsewhere and not only in the United Kingdom. Today there are Fifteens working in Melbourne and Amsterdam. Although they operate under different management, the overseas Fifteens work broadly according to the same principles as the London mother ship. Put simply, if they carry the Fifteen moniker, there must be a commitment to training a set number of teenagers every year.

The Fifteen brand has been rolled out through franchise agreements. The principle is a simple one. Each franchisee pays an upfront fee and an annual royalty based on a percentage of profit to the Fifteen Foundation in return for the right to use the name and logos and recipes of the London operation. As part of the Fifteen family, franchised restaurants also benefit from centralized PR.

In common with most well-run franchise operations, the Fifteens in Cornwall, Amsterdam and Melbourne must also agree to adhere to the brand values of the Oliver original. For instance, the look and feel of the establishments must be contemporary and the locations trendy. In addition, the franchisees must offer similar menus to those available in London and there is (naturally enough) an insistence on using the best possible ingredients. Beyond those broad guidelines, the franchise operators are free to put their own touches to the Fifteen brand.

Winning a Fifteen franchise isn't easy. By 2006 around 2000 organizations had applied to open a Fifteen restaurant and at that stage only Amsterdam and Cornwall had been successful. That's not surprising. Applicants must undergo thorough vetting to ensure their own principles are in line with those of Oliver and his colleagues on the Fifteen Foundation board. Equally important, the vetting process is intended to ensure that applicants will have access to the necessary finance and support from local organizations. Once up and running, the local operations must return an agreed sum to the centre. As *The Guardian* newspaper's Alison Benjamin reported in 2006, Amsterdam had agreed to pay 150,000 euros per year or 30% of its gross product, depending on which sum was larger.

FROM SOCIAL ENTERPRISE TO INTERNATIONAL BUSINESS

The strictures placed upon Fifteen's franchise holders reflect the nature of the enterprise. Running a Fifteen restaurant is not only a business opportunity, it is an opportunity to do good in the world. As such, those who take up the challenge have to combine the business skills necessary to open and maintain a cool contemporary restaurant with a genuine commitment to working with disadvantaged young people and improving their lot. Despite plans for a wider roll out, there are currently just four Fifteen restaurants dotted around the globe and we shouldn't expect the brand to be rivalling the ubiquity of Starbucks at any time in the near future.

Oliver has taken the franchise model and also applied it to his fully commercial restaurant concept Jamie's Italian.

In the UK the Jamie's Italian chain is still at the very early stages of its development. With branches in just six locations – Bath, Oxford, Guildford, Brighton, Kingston and London's Canary Wharf – the chain still has lot of territory to conquer if it is to fully capitalize on the strength of the Oliver brand. That's not surprising. It costs a lot of money to start a restaurant. Even if the Jamie logo above the door guarantees that the revenues will come rolling in, the process of planning, finding a location, recruiting staff and building a customer base eats cash. Expansion tends to be on a step by step basis.

But Oliver's ambitions for Jamie's Italian extend well beyond the UK. In August 2009 it was announced that Oliver planned to launch no less than 30 of the restaurants across Asia.

The plans are ambitious. Driven by rising interest in Italian food, the first wave will see six restaurants opening in Hong Kong and China. This will be followed by a second wave of 24 across the wider region. Kevin Bacon, managing director of Jamie's Italian International was bullish about the move. 'Ultimately with Jamie's Italian, it works; it's special and it has an appeal that could translate to just about any city in the world'.

Why Asia? For one thing, the rise of the Asian tiger economies and, more recently, the emergence of both India and China as major economic powers, have created a young middle class with a hunger to sample the good things in life. This interest has been fuelled by Oliver's own TV programmes, which are widely shown in the region.

But taking a business that has barely left the starting blocks and scaling it up around the world is a huge undertaking. Kevin Bacon made clear that the company would be looking for help. 'When it comes to going international, we want to do it with partners', he said, 'Partners who share our ethos and who want to grow alongside our ethos.'

In the case of Asia, the partner is Tranic Franchising – a specialist provider of franchising and licensing services. Under the deal as it stands, the partners will open a number of 'company owned' restaurants. With the brand established, further expansion will be via licensing to franchisees. Tranic – as the partner on the ground – will provide the day-to-day management of all the licensing arrangements in the region.

'I am the first cookery programme ever to be sold to France, Italy, Spain. I'm in 34 different countries on 60 channels. I do all the big name chat shows in America and I have a lot of sweeping up to do when I get over there.'

Even under license/franchise agreements there's a lot of money at stake. Tranic has indicated that it wants to establish Hong Kong as a hub for training and, to cover initial start-up costs, the company was seeking to raise around $US200m. And Asia could be just the first step. Edward Pinshaw, chairman of Tranic has indicated that the next step could be a roll out in Europe.

THE PERILS OF INTERNATIONAL EXPANSION

In seeking out partners with experience on the ground, Oliver and his company have sought to address some of the key issues that face businesses as they make the transition from domestic to international players.

Thanks to the internet, just about anyone can sell internationally. If you're based in Aberdeen or Cardiff but have a product that appeals to a customer in New York or Tokyo, taking an order and shipping the goods presents no real problem – as long as you have a merchants account with a credit card company and the technology to process a transaction.

Establishing a genuine international presence is notoriously more difficult. Let's say you have a product with global appeal. Yes, you can sell one or two – maybe even one or two hundred – via the internet, but its unlikely that you'll establish any real traction in an overseas market.

The pitfalls are numerous. From the comfort of an office in the UK, you may think you have a market in France, the US or Hong Kong. But the view from the ground may look very different. Unless you know who the local players are you could well find yourself spending a huge amount of time, money and energy pursuing customers in a market that is already saturated with well-established competitors.

Then there are the cultural pitfalls. Even within Europe, customer attitudes vary enormously. For instance, in Britain we've long been hooked on credit cards. We use them without thinking and all too often pay the price in terms of burgeoning debt. In France or Germany, debit and charge cards rule supreme. A small difference, perhaps, but one that you're going to have to understand in order to trade successfully.

Then there is the cost of setting up a presence on the ground. If you're going to market your business successfully in any territory, the chances are that you'll need to work proactively and appropriately to get the message across to the local audience. Often that means setting up an office to handle not only the marketing but the customer service functions. That in turn takes you into the complex area of local employment law.

Small wonder then, that many businesses consider selling into one or more overseas markets, only to decide against it when they examine the costs and risks.

Even the strongest brands can find going international a bridge too far. Witness Marks & Spencer's failure in the French market, and consequent retreat. Arguably, setting up a restaurant business is one of the riskiest strategies of all. Put simply, the world is awash with restaurants.

But there are ways and means to reduce the risk. One of the most effective is to establish a partnership – usually a joint venture – with a complementary business that knows the territory. The complementary fit is important. There are those who'll argue that joint ventures have a propensity to come to grief because they're all too often based on an uneasy alliance of two or more firms that have the ambition to expand internationally but who lack the resources to do it alone. They set up management structures, pool cash and resources and set about exploiting the market in question. The problem is that, at heart, the management of each company would rather be going it alone. Over time, the relationship goes sour and the venture falters.

Things tend to work better when the parties bring different but complementary skillsets. That appears to be the case in the Oliver/ Tranic relationship. One party has local knowledge and experience of the franchise trade in the area. The other has a killer brand and a clear view of what the restaurants should look and feel like and the niche they will fill in the market. It remains to be seen how successful Oliver's international ventures will prove, but the combination of partnership and a franchise model has worked well for others in the past.

EXPORT THE FORMAT

Oliver's television career has also taken a new international direction through an agreement to produce a series of six programmes specifically for the US market.

Produced by Fresh One and US company Ryan Searcrest Productions, the show follows Oliver on an odyssey to Huntingdon West Virginia, a town recognized as one of the most obese and unhealthy in the entire USA. During his stay there, Oliver attempts to persuade and encourage the populace to adopt a healthier diet.

If this all sounds terribly familiar, it should do. The programme takes its cue from *Jamie's School Dinners* and *Jamie's Ministry of Food*. Neatly pulling the themes of both those shows into a seamless whole for the US, he goes into schools with the aim of improving menus and takes his good food message to the wider community.

As in the UK, he has his work cut out. According to the Centre for Disease Control and Pollution, around half the population of the Huntingdon-Ashland Metropolitan district are officially obese, and the area has the highest incidence of heart disease and diabetes in the US. To emphasize the point, in one of Oliver's early encounters – as reported in the *New York Times* – is an eight year old child suffering from type 2 diabetes and carrying 80 lbs more than her recommended weight.

On the face of it, it was a brave choice for a show. The US networks had been after him for some time and it would probably have been easier to sign up for a recipe show. Instead, he's chosen to take on a food culture characterized in Huntingdon by the town's famous fifteen pound burger. And given the controversy that surrounded his bid to encourage the people of Rotherham, Yorkshire to improve their diet, he must have known that pulling off the same trick in a foreign country was fraught with pitfalls. After all, why should the people of a US town with a 19% poverty rate welcome the attentions of an English celebrity chef?

In the US alone, he's swapped comic lines with the likes of chat show hosts David Letterman and Jay Leno and swapped cookery tips with national treasure Oprah Winfrey. He's even shared a screen (and a grill pan) with Tom Cruise

However, the formula is tried and tested, and Oliver has a track record of charming people away from deep fried food and into a world of fresh, low fat ingredients. And as he's demonstrated in the UK, he's also a reality TV natural.

Nor is it kicking against the political grain. Health is at the centre of the Obama government's political agenda and there is a drive to improve nutritional standards in schools and communities.

The US shows follow in a long tradition of UK and European reality shows successfully adapted for the US market. Perhaps the biggest hits in this genre have come from the stable of pop TV mogul, Simon Cowell. *America's Got Talent* (the child of *Britain's Got Talent*) and *American Idol* (a *Pop Idol/X Factor* clone) have wowed US audiences while remaining familiar to anyone who has seen the British originals. They've also made US stars of Cowell himself and Piers Morgan. Aware that he is walking the same road, Oliver has admitted calling Cowell to ask for advice before starting work on his US show.

Oliver has taken the franchise model and applied it to his fully commercial restaurant concept Jamie's Italian

If the US show proves a success, doubtless it will be re-exported back to the UK, underlining his global bankability. TV is his home turf, but the really interesting question over the next few years will centre on how successful ventures such as Jamie's Italian are. Will his celebrity provide the leverage to create a truly international restaurant chain? Watch this space.

GO INTERNATIONAL

Oliver's status as an international phenomenon was confirmed early in his career but, in addition to enjoying the financial benefits of global sales for his TV shows and books, he has also capitalized on his fame by launching business ventures in overseas markets. This is how he did it.

- **Make a name for yourself.** In the early part of his career, Oliver's global marketing work was mostly done for him by the BBC's commercial arm. *The Naked Chef* TV series was sold to more than 60 countries, including the epicenter of gastronomy, France. Thanks to TV success his books also became global best-sellers.

- **Put in the work.** However, Oliver was more than happy to promote his own cause. As in the UK he hit the chat show circuit. In the US he proved himself more than capable of holding his own in the company of David Letterman, Jay Leno and Oprah Winfrey.

- **Franchise your business idea.** When the Fifteen Restaurant opened in London, there was a huge amount of interest in its social enterprise model. To date, the Fifteen Foundation set up by Oliver has granted franchises to teams in Cornwall, Amsterdam and Melbourne. Fifteen-branded restaurants are now operating in those cities and franchisees pay a fee to the London based Fifteen Foundation and an annual royalty.

- **Secure the brand values.** Franchisees must adhere to the guiding principle of Fifteen while also sticking to broad guidelines on look and feel, location, and menus.

- **Extend the franchise approach.** Oliver's Jamie's Italian company is planning to roll out restaurants bearing that name across Asia.

- **Work with local partners.** The company has partnered with Tranic Franchising, a business with experience in licensing and franchising in the Asian market.

- **Make programmes for specific markets.** Oliver is now making series in the US, with US subject matter. His first venture mirrors the reality TV approach pioneered by *Jamie's Kitchen* and *Ministry of Food*.

8

PROTECT THE BRAND

To the casual observer he's a television star with a nice side-line in cookery books. To anyone who chooses to take a closer look, Oliver is the figurehead of an increasingly complex business organization. After the TV shows and books came advertising contracts with Sainsbury's, the establishment of a TV production company, a string of retail ventures and, of course, the restaurants. Even in the midst of a deep recession he continued to recruit more staff and launch new ventures. Oliver the man and Oliver the brand represent a genuine business success story.

But here's the tricky bit. Jamie Oliver now employs a lot of people to run his businesses and this raises a question. When a business empire is based around the personality of one man, how do you ensure that it retains the brand values as the organization grows?

This is not an issue that is unique to Oliver. Young businesses are usually shaped by the personality and vision of their founders. With maybe a handful of staff servicing a limited number of customers, it's relatively easy for an entrepreneur or a tightly knit management team to keep a close check on everything. They probably talk to the big customers, sit in on sales meetings and even turn the lights out when everyone else has gone home. As the business grows, it changes. More staff, more customers, more product or service lines equate to greater complexity. It's no longer possible for the founders to run the show unaided. They have to bring in department heads and give them real responsibility. Further down the line, the chances are they'll have to buy in some expensive specialist talent. Perhaps a marketing director to free up the managing director to do other things. Or a finance director to replace the humble bookkeeper. All these people leave their mark and, before long, the culture of the company begins to evolve.

The bigger and more diverse a business becomes, the harder it is to hold on to the corporate culture and the original brand values. New products or business ventures can be a fast track to higher revenues but they can also confuse the public. To return to Oliver's home turf, let's say a celebrated restaurateur decides to put his name to a range of ready meals. In theory, retaining a single brand name could be a good idea. Those who know the restaurant chain may be attracted to the packages on the supermarket shelves. That recognition factor could mean a big saving on the marketing budget.

On the media side, he is clearly the star of the show and while he works with a range of partners to produce and distribute his work, he is at the centre of developing ideas and formats

But here's the rub. The experience of buying a ready meal from a supermarket is going to be very different from that of eating out. A company that gives its name to both of these products must ensure that – at some level – there is a consistent brand message. Equally important, the quality of one experience should reflect the quality of the other.

That can be hard to achieve. For one thing, the consumer will be making judgements on two very different products. The two ventures will probably have their own management teams, each struggling to market one set of products while preserving a brand relationship with the sister business.

In this respect, expansion and diversification is as much about brand management as it is about the mechanics of raising finance, opening new offices and outlets or recruiting staff. So how has Oliver grown his business while protecting the integrity of his brand?

COMPANY STRUCTURE

It's worth taking a close look at how the Oliver empire is structured.

Reflecting the range of his commercial affairs, Oliver and wife Jools have registered a diverse group of companies as vehicles for their business interests. Most of these operate under the umbrella of Jamie Oliver Holdings.

Beneath the holding company we then have Jamie Oliver Limited, which handles his publishing, TV presenting services, live shows and his advertising relationship with Sainsbury's.

Then there is Jamie Oliver Enterprises, a company that holds stakes in a range of brand management related businesses. These include the Flour Station bakery, Fresh One, his TV production company, Fresh Crush, the business that markets his Flavour Shaker product, and Web design company the Plant.

In addition there is Fresh Partners (a talent management agency) and Jools Enterprises, a publishing company.

All the above funnel their profits back through Jamie Oliver Holdings, but there are also a number of businesses that operate independently of the holding company. These include the increasingly important Fresh Venture Holdings (operating as Fresh Retail) and the Jamie's Italian chain. Sitting out on a limb – as social enterprise – is the Fifteen Foundation and associated restaurants.

On an outer orbit, we have a community of partners – third party businesses that have a close association with Oliver and his various ventures. The most famous of these – thanks to the chef's long-standing advertising/endorsement deal – is the Sainsbury's super-market group. The chef also has product licensing deals with man-ufactures such as Tefal (kitchenware), Royal Worcester (ceramics), Merison (barbeque tools) and DKB Household (the Jamie Oliver Flavour Shaker). Media partners include Freemantle (distribution of TV programmes and DVDs) and Penguin (book publishing).

There are good reasons to break up a diversifying business into stand-alone components under a holding company. It makes management easier. Rather than having a range of enterprises under a monolithic company structure, you have a number of semi-autonomous ventures, each with a clear mission statement and their own management teams.

Equally important, you take some of the financial risk out of the expansion process. For instance, if one business fails or goes through a bad patch, its problems will clearly impact on the rev-enue that is fed through the holding company. However, its financial difficulties should be containable within the structure of that particular business. If a non-performing business fails, it can be liquidated without impacting on the other companies within the group. Nevertheless, there is nothing to stop the owners and directors of these companies lending or investing cash in other businesses within the group, so wealthy, established businesses can finance start-ups or ventures in need of further investment.

STAY IN CONTROL

There are of course control issues that need to be addressed. The growth of a business inevitably involves the owners and founders losing a certain degree of their influence over events, at least in terms of day-to-day management. To get the best out of senior staff you need to give them some autonomy, and this can be a difficult pill to swallow.

Oliver's approach to recruitment mirrors his own work ethic and commitment. He likes to surround himself with talented and inspiring people who do a good job and who are comfortable trying fresh ideas and pursuing new ventures

It could mean the head of a marketing, sales or accounts team making their own hiring decisions rather than referring everything back up to the person in charge. Many owner/managers are relieved to devolve that kind of responsibility, especially when the business gets to a certain size. But what if an expensive and newly acquired marketing manager lobbies hard to reposition a brand that has been lovingly nurtured by the founder? These are issues that can cause a huge amount of tension. Arguably they are more likely to emerge in a group structure where the founder's time is stretched thin.

Analysis of Oliver's business empire suggests that he continues to run a tight ship, especially in core parts of the business. On the media side, he is clearly the star of the show and while he works with a range of partners to produce and distribute his work, he is at the centre of developing ideas and formats.

Elsewhere in the business, he is a hands-on owner, particularly in the case of ventures that are key to the maintenance of his public reputation. Witness Fresh Retail, the Manchester-based company set up to develop and market Oliver-branded products from sauces and oils to kitchenware. Here Oliver is a major shareholder and continues to take an active interest in developing products, sourcing suppliers and positioning of the brand. This includes a policy of including personalized messages on the labelling of Fresh One products. [1]

Fresh Retail works with a range of partners, such as the aforementioned Tefal and Royal Worcester, with many products being marketed under licence. This effectively brings two brands together, running the risk that one will dilute the other; someone buying a set of non-stick saucepans will be getting products flying the twin flags of Oliver and Tefal. But in this case, the co-existence of the two brands works rather well: one has an established reputation for quality, and the other is known as an ambassador for good British cooking.

In fact, the range is pretty much reflective of the Oliver brand. On the Tefal website, the Oliver section, with its videos and messages from Jamie, looks uncannily similar to the content and style on his own web pages. In effect this means that his own branding has another route to market via Tefal's marketing channels.

Meanwhile, Fresh One – the TV production company that is vital to Oliver's success – is 100% under his control, as is Jools Enterprises, and he has an 88.5% stake in Jamie's Italian.

Majority stakes are not necessarily the rule. In the case of businesses such as the Plant (web design) and Fresh Partners (talent agency), he and Jools are content to hold minority stakes of around 20%. Arguably these companies are far less important to the maintenance of Oliver's brand equity than Fresh One or Fresh Retail.

CHOOSE THE RIGHT PEOPLE

But holding a majority stake in a company shouldn't mean appointing paper tigers as managers or senior staff. To succeed, businesses need talented and motivated employees, from the most junior starter to senior managers. Oliver is very aware of this both in terms of his stated business philosophy and his record on appointments.

Oliver's approach to recruitment mirrors his own work ethic and commitment. He likes to surround himself with talented and inspiring people who do a good job and who are prepared to try new things. He is not impressed by those who fail to step up to the plate. 'I'm not interested in people getting pissed on a Sunday night and coming to me on a Monday when I'm paying their wage', he told *The Guardian* in 2005. 'If you want doors to open, then I'll open them for you, but you've gotta be a rock, you gotta be consistent, every day, day in, day out.'[2]

Employing high flyers as managers is about more than putting the day-to-day management growing business in safe hands. They bring in expertise in their chosen industries, coupled with their own managerial skills

And he can still be hands-on in the recruitment process, even at the furthest outposts of his empire. Witness his Ministry of Food venture – in parallel with the television programme, Oliver and his team set up a kitchen in Rotherham, Yorkshire, with the aim of teaching local people to cook. The intention was to fund the project through his own organization in the first instance, before eventually handing it over to the local council to run as a community project. But even with the handover in sight, he was wary of the impact that local officials taking over might have on his brand.

'The reason the Ministry is working in Rotherham is because we went up there and interviewed 30 local boys and girls, and we're not fucking stupid. If they [local government] did it, can you imagine what the staff would look like? You could have anyone getting a fucking job', he said in 2008.[3]

HIRE TOP TOP TALENT

Oliver has not been slow to recruit big hitters into all parts of his organization and work with strong personalities.

As a programme maker has worked closely with Dominique Walker, a commissioning editor at Channel 4 and series producer on *Jamie's School Dinners*. Oliver knows when to delegate to other people. 'The thing about Jamie is he spots talents, recognises what everyone else's strengths are and then lets you do what you're good at', she told *The Guardian* in 2006 before going on to describe the freedom she was allowed to make the programme. 'Jamie didn't come and see the [*School Dinners*] edit until it had been signed off by C4. His attitude was "you tell me what you need." He understood we needed great TV moments, as programme makers'.[4]

Away from the camera, Oliver has appointed expert managers to run his businesses. They have included David Page, formerly managing director of Indian food company Patak. He joined Oliver's Fresh Retail Ventures in 2007. Talking to *The Grocer* magazine, he wasted no time in signalling his plans to take the company on a fast growth curve. 'It's fair to call Fresh Retail Ventures a small business but I'd like to think we can double its size every two to three years', Page said. 'The board and Jamie Oliver believe I've got the experience to help the young team develop.'[5]

As we saw earlier in the book, Oliver's TV production company also has an experienced hand at the helm. Recruited from Diverse Productions – a key supplier of programmes to Channel 4, Roy Ackerman joined Fresh One with a brief to diversify from a portfolio of shows that were largely created around Oliver. That could ultimately mean some radical departures for Fresh One. With his feet under the table Ackerman began working on programmes that included a documentary, a drama and further cookery pro-grammes featuring new talent.

Meanwhile, over on the social enterprise side of the business, respected social entrepreneur Liam Black has been replaced by an equally experienced Penny Newman as CEO of Fifteen. Black built on Oliver's idea by expanding the franchise into Europe and Aus-tralia. Newman aims to increase the scope of the training on offer through the Fifteen Foundation.

Employing high flyers as managers is about more than putting the day-to-day management growing business in safe hands. They bring in expertise in their chosen industries, coupled with their own managerial skills. They also make a business more sustain-able and in some cases saleable. The shelf life of Oliver's media ventures is largely dependent on his own willingness to go on making TV programmes and writing books. When he stops, the flow of material to television and into print will inevitably dry up. But companies such as Fresh One, Fresh Retail and Jamie's Italian potentially have a much longer shelf life, independent of Oliver's TV presence.

The proviso is that they need good people in charge, people who can both move the businesses forward and deliver on the brand proposition.

PARTNERS

If staff and managers bring talent and expertise into the business via the front door, partnerships import skills via the tradesman's entrance. For the most part, Oliver's companies are marketing businesses. They develop, source and design products then sell them – in one way or another – to the public at large. And while Oliver owns – or part owns – the means of production in the case of Fresh One, his restaurants and the Flour Station, manufacturing requires a different set of skills.

The mission statement is very clear. Jamie Oliver and his companies aim to 'help as many people as possible eat better food and live a better life'[6]

Hence the presence of a brace of partnerships, with companies such as Tefal, Merison, Royal Worcester, and William Levene DKB. These are household names in their own right, each with a long tradition of manufacturing and quality. Indeed, in the case of Royal Worcester – producer of Oliver-branded ceramics – that history stretches back more than 250 years.

Not all of Oliver's business partners are quite so venerable. One of his latest ventures is a series of video recipe shows, conceived and designed to be played on mobile phones. While Fresh One shoots the material, mobile content provider Inventa supplies the technical expertise in the delivery of the footage to handsets. Mobile content is a young industry but, as with his other partnerships, Oliver has chosen to work with a company that has already made a mark. In its short life, Inventa has produced more than 200 shows for mobile phones and the internet, picking up a string of awards in the process. With DJ Pete Tong among the founders, it also has some of the star appeal that characterizes Oliver's own business portfolio.

There are always potential pitfalls when two brands come together in a partnership. As a business owner you will be in total control of the face that your company and its brand presents to the wider world. If there are problems with quality, customer service or the positioning of the brand, you'll be able to take action to put things right. Things can get a lot trickier when you bring partners on board. Let's say you team up with a manufacturer to bring a new range of products to the market under your company's name. If the goods aren't manufactured in line with expectations of the consumer, it will be your company's brand rather than that of the manufacturer that takes a hit. The same is true if you outsource your customer service function to a call centre provider. If the phone operatives are indifferent, negligent or simply fail to follow up on customer queries, then your brand will suffer.

Of course, you try to strip out as much risk from these arrangements as possible through contracts that lay down the law on quality and service. Arguably Oliver has also 'de-risked' his own partnership agreements by signing alliances with long established names, which brings all the advantages of co-branding. In the alliance with Tefal, both parties have reputations to protect, and both have a lot to gain from a successful relationship. Oliver gains an additional income stream by licensing his name. Tefal benefits from Oliver's popularity and gains a point of differentiation from its competitors.

THE FRANCHISEES

As Oliver grows his restaurant chain in Britain and around the world, franchising is set to become much more important. We've already seen how London's Fifteen restaurant has been replicated in Cornwall, Melbourne and Amsterdam through a franchise agreement. As Jamie's Italian prepares to open its first restaurants in Asia, plans for expansion across that region are based around a mix of company owned and franchised businesses.

The principle of franchising – or to be more precise, business format franchising – are well known. When a company builds a brand, a business model and a trading method, that format can be licensed to third parties.

These third party licensees aren't employees. Typically they form their own companies or retain self-employed status and are responsible for generating sales and profits. They will run the franchised operations as their own businesses, while adhering to the trading practices and brand values dictated by the company that has granted the licence. In return for the right to trade under the brand, they will usually pay an upfront fee and an annual royalty based on profits.

Franchising offers businesses with a strong brand an opportunity to scale up rapidly, either nationally or internationally. Let's take the example of a restaurant chain with five or six establishments operating under a single brand and 100% owned by one company. If that chain wants to expand further it faces the prospect of raising money, finding premises and employing new staff.

However, if the brand is strong enough, the alternative is to sell the franchise to someone who will a) pay money up front for the licence and b) take responsibility for renting premises and taking on staff. Thus the upfront cost of expansion is neatly inverted into an upfront revenue opportunity.

But there are hazards. If the franchise model is to work, you have to find the right partners – essentially individuals with the skills to take your business model and make a success of it in their own chosen location. They need to demonstrate an understanding of the business model and respect the brand values. They must also have the financial wherewithal to undertake the necessary investment in the business.

But the brand owner also has a role to play in supporting franchisees. Generally speaking, most of the marketing material comes from the mother company and successful franchisors also provide comprehensive training and logistical support to their partners.

Oliver and his team have already demonstrated a solid grasp of the do's and don'ts of franchising. Applicants for Fifteen franchises were carefully vetted to ensure they had the correct values to take on a high-profile social venture, plus the business skills and access to finance necessary to start and run sustainable restaurants with a commitment to training.

Meanwhile, plans to license the Jamie's Italian chain across Asia have been carefully laid. The UK company has partnered with Tranic Franchising, a licensing specialist with experience in rolling out businesses in the region. In addition to identifying and selecting licence partners, Tranic will also work with Jamie's Italian to establish a training and business support centre in Hong Kong. Over the next few years we'll see whether this structure will enable the Jamie's Italian chain to address a very different marketplace from that of the UK while retaining the elements that have made it a success in Britain. [7]

A CLEAR MISSION

As the Oliver portfolio of businesses expands, it's vital that employees and partners have a clear sense of what Oliver the man is setting out to achieve.

The mission statement is very clear. Jamie Oliver and his companies aim to 'help as many people as possible eat better food and live a better life'.[8] It's a commitment that neatly embraces everything from recipe books through to branded kitchenware.

There are secondary goals too. According to the official guide to his business activities, Oliver's companies operate according to three guiding principles.[9]

1   They should be creative, with staff always ready to embrace new ideas. That not only means a readiness to design and market new products but also a commitment to provide better service and improve the business.

2   Oliver has made sustainability a priority. All ventures within the group should be commercially viable and, over time, become less dependent on 'Jamie the person' and more dependent on 'Jamie the brand'.

3   Oliver has decreed that wherever possible his companies should demonstrate a 'big social heart' while maintaining a commitment to quality and integrity.

These are powerful values and the ongoing strength of Oliver's business activities will depend on his ability to embed them at all levels of the organization.

PROTECT THE BRAND

To date, Jamie Oliver has succeeded in creating a multi-headed business empire, without undermining public perception of 'Oliver the man', or the brand he has created. This is how he has done it.

- **Choose good people.** Oliver is committed to employing energetic and creative people. At the managerial level, he hires people with broad experience of the sectors in which they operate.
- **Choose effective partners.** Oliver has teamed up with a number of market leaders to sell branded products under licence. These include Tefal, Royal Worcester, Merison and DKB Household. By using long-established reputable companies as manufacturing partners he is putting his own brand in safe hands.
- **Stay in control.** Jamie Oliver owns and part owns a network of companies. By retaining majority ownership in those that are central to his brand and the way it is perceived, he is in a strong position to shape their development and protect his brand equity.
- **Have a mission.** Oliver has stated clearly the overarching principles that guide his business ventures.

9

BE CONTROVERSIAL

Jamie Oliver once described himself as a 'professional stirrer', and as self-penned thumbnail sketches go, it wasn't far off the mark.

Throughout his career in the public eye he has been a controversial and divisive figure. In the early days the controversies were for the most part small-scale and trivial – normally centred around the question of whether Oliver was a natural TV performer or an industrial-strength pain with a mouth that ran well ahead of his brain.

Certainly the adage 'think before you speak' was not one that the early Oliver appeared to be aware of. In a TV world where presenters at least paid lip-service to the concept of political correctness, he would cheerfully refer to wife Jools as his 'his missus', and recall their first meeting by enthusiastically describing the impact of her 'Bristol cities' on his adolescent mind.

Truth to tell, his political incorrectness did him little harm. For everyone who cringed at his loose way with words, there were others who applauded his authenticity and declared him a breath of fresh air in a TV cookery universe that was still largely dominated by middle-class niceties.

His fans were also prepared to forgive him his accent – described by critics as 'mockney' (mock cockney) – and the incessant use of the word 'pukka' to describe just about every recipe that escaped from his kitchen. It was a word, he explained, that was used widely in Essex. Thus his fans could be further assured that Oliver was the real deal – the confident and authentic product of a Britain where regional diversity in accent and vocabulary enriched the nation. Meanwhile, his detractors buried their faces in their hands – or switched to another channel.

But as his career developed, Oliver was prepared to embrace real controversy over issues such as the food we feed our children in and out of schools, and the welfare of animals. More than that, controversy became part of his persona as a TV performer. The more controversial he became, the more his stature and his TV ratings grew. He was not just a 'stirrer' – he was a 'professional stirrer', and one that had a real impact on people's lives.

GRAB THE NETTLE

The emergence of Oliver the 'stirrer' really began with *Jamie's School Dinners* on Channel 4 television. Like its predecessor, *Jamie's Kitchen*, it was a series that combined Oliver's enthusiasm for food with a socially useful agenda.

But there was a difference. In *Jamie's Kitchen*, Oliver had undertaken the massive task of taking a group of unemployed – and sometimes underprivileged – teenagers and moulding them into trained chefs who would be capable of working at the best restaurants in the land.

In public and political opinion, Oliver wasn't stepping on anyone's toes. Who could challenge the notion that training up the unemployed to go into gainful employment is anything other than a good thing?

The only controversy this programme courted was centred around the question that dogs just about all reality TV programmes – is what you see on screen real, or artifice? Questions were asked about those taking part. Were the trainees really comprised of genuinely underprivileged people or were they just regular teenagers, handpicked to make the programme work? The first series was mainly peopled by teenagers who simply happened to be jobless rather than people with serious problems, but they were unemployed, they did want to work and Oliver was prepared to help them.

Jamie's School Dinners was a different bunch of bananas. Oliver was appalled at the standard of food served in school canteens all over Britain. Equally important, he believed that improving the quality of the food on offer would enhance the lives of pupils, improve behaviour and enhance learning ability.

The emergence of Oliver the 'stirrer' really began with *Jamie's School Dinners* **on Channel 4 television. Like its predecessor,** *Jamie's Kitchen*, **it was a series that combined Oliver's enthusiasm for food with a socially useful agenda**

But in highlighting the shortcomings of school meals, Oliver was challenging a hornet's nest of pre-conceptions and vested interests. Lining up against him in no particular order were the hard-pressed dinner ladies who, initially at least, resented being told how to do their jobs. Then there were the pupils who preferred chips over carrots any day. Certain sections of the food industry, particularly those who supplied schools and local authorities, were less than happy too. And Oliver was casting a forensic light on a hitherto murky area of government policy. Concerns over the quality of school meals had been kicked into touch by successive governments. Politicians at national and local level had no interest in retrieving those concerns.

TAKE ON THE ESTABLISHMENT

Now for some entrepreneurs – Richard Branson being the best known case in point – taking on the big guys is what business life is all about. Indeed, as his Virgin Empire grew from its music-focused origins to embrace planes, trains, soft drinks, personal finance, online gaming, television and a host of other things, the common factor that linked these diverse activities together was his readiness for a fight.

A common Virgin strategy is to identify a lucrative market dominated by big players. Then the company launches a business against the incumbents. As it's a Virgin business, the chances are it will present a value-for-money, 'cooler' face to consumers than its established rivals. Sometimes it works, sometimes it doesn't, but the David vs Goliath scenario is an important part of how the public sees Virgin. It is a challenger brand. It can be a great place for an entrepreneur to be.

But at this stage Oliver was not an entrepreneur in the accepted sense – he was a television presenter on a mission. This in itself can be a good career move. As documentary maker Michael Moore would doubtless testify, a willingness to take on the establishment – whether in the form of big business or government – can be a career-building attribute. You're standing up for the little guy, making a difference, and building your reputation.

Oliver wasn't a journalist or documentary film maker. But he did own his own production company and had clear ideas about the kind of TV he wanted to make. He also had the confidence to pitch his own opinions against the received wisdom of what was possible in the confines of a school canteen.

By taking on major vested interests and courting controversy, he had strengthened his own reputation.

GO AGAINST THE GRAIN

The school dinners campaign dropped Oliver into the centre of a realm that had largely been forgotten about or ignored by politicians, and even parents, for a long time.

The history looked like this. Free school meals were introduced in 1906 by a Liberal government. To be more precise, the legislation passed at the beginning of the twentieth century allowed but did not compel local authorities to provide dinners for the children attending their schools. As a result, there was not a coordinated policy.

All that changed in the 1940s when it became government policy to ensure that all schools would offer meals that accounted for 40% of the daily protein requirement of each child. That was the start of what some would see as a 'golden age' for school meals.

That golden age came to a juddering halt when a Conservative government under Margaret Thatcher effectively privatized the school meals service. The Conservatives were keen both to cut public spending and provide new markets for private sector businesses. In line with that twin objective, the 1980s Education Act removed the obligation of local authorities to provide school meals at a fixed price. Dinners didn't disappear from schools, but the focus on nutrition certainly did. Some local authorities brought in private contractors who could use their economies of scale to reduce the cost per meal. Others dropped the service completely, except for the provision of packed lunches for those entitled to

free school meals. A third group kept control of the
school meals service while struggling with
the pressure to keep costs down. Increas-   **… Oliver's school**
ingly, schools introduced pay-as-you-eat   **dinners campaign was**
cafeterias. Rather than parents paying a   **out of keeping with the**
weekly or monthly sum guaranteeing a   **supposed spirit of the**
meal every day, children brought in cash   **times. In an era when**
and chose from a self-service menu.   **consumer choice was**
                                                                                king, he was going
As a result, there was pressure to keep   **against the grain**
the 'customers' satisfied: keeping prices
low and giving them what they wanted. Of
course, children and teenagers aren't always the best
judges of what's good for them. Give them a pizza or a piece of
reconstituted meat primed with an addictive mix of salt and sugar
and they're more than happy.

The changes in the school meals system happened under the
watch of a Conservative government but when Oliver began his
campaign for better food the Labour party was in charge. In theory,
a party that had pledged to improve education and (more generally) living standards should have embraced Oliver's campaign to
improve school dinners from the outset, but the politics was com-
plicated.

Under Tony Blair, the party had become – publicly at least – a cham-
pion of consumer choice. Labour pledged to improve much-loved
state institutions such as the NHS and the education system while
at the same time remaining free-market friendly. The government
was wary of any accusation that it was impinging on the choices
made by individuals. It was determined to demonstrate that the
words 'Labour party' and 'nanny state' were not synonymous.

In that respect, Oliver's school dinners campaign was out of keeping with the spirit of the times. In an era when consumer choice was king, he was going against the grain. He was showing what the government was initially unwilling to acknowledge, that parents and children sometimes don't know best.

Once again he divided the nation. On the one hand he was applauded by teachers and parents who dealt daily with the impact of sugar and additives on child behaviour. On the other, there were parents who clearly resented an 'elitist foodie' interfering with their children's diets, or criticizing their choices.

BE OUTSPOKEN AND SET THE AGENDA

Nor was he popular with the food industry. One of the most iconic moments in Oliver's school dinners campaign was his public critique of the infamous Turkey Twizzler.

When Oliver began shooting the *Jamie's School Dinners* series, Turkey Twizzlers were something of a favourite with young consumers, despite containing relatively small amounts of real meat (around 34%) and a lot of fat, sugar, coating and additives. Incensed by what he saw as junk food fed to children on an almost daily basis, Oliver used the unfortunate product as a stick with which to beat what he saw as the irresponsible school meals industry.

The company producing the Twizzler bravely attempted to limit the damage. In a statement issued to the BBC's *Newsround* programme the company said: 'Turkey Twizzlers can be part of a balanced diet', adding 'This seems to be getting silly and out of hand. The fat levels have already been reduced but even prior to that were less than in an average sausage. Is Jamie really saying that sausages are off the menu too?'[1]

But the damage had already been done. Faced with a wave of public indignation generated by Oliver's TV campaigning, two of the major private sector companies supplying school meals quickly decided that it was time to wake up and smell the coffee. Scolarest and Sodexho announced very publicly that Turkey Twizzlers would be off the menu.

While Jamie Oliver's TV career flourished, his campaigns were affecting major employers. For instance, in 2006 catering company Compass, owner of the Scolarest, blamed the Jamie Oliver effect for a sharp drop in profits

While the Twizzler disappeared from school menus, it was still widely available in supermarkets and in the aftermath of 'Twizzlergate', sales of the meat product soared by a third. Nevertheless, Oliver had proved a point. By being outspoken and revealing exactly what goes into cheap food products, he was setting an agenda. It was an agenda to which the industry felt it had to respond, even if consumer habits were harder to change. In the end, Bernard Matthews also bowed to the Oliver agenda. In 2005, the Twizzler went out of production. So far it has not been revived.

And, of course, there are consequences to all this. While Jamie Oliver's TV career flourished, his campaigns were affecting major employers. For instance, in 2006 catering company Compass, owner of the Scolarest, blamed the Jamie Oliver effect for a sharp drop in profits as its schools division struggled to get to grips with the healthy eating agenda that Oliver had begun. Indeed, in 2006 the *Financial Times* reported: 'Last year, operating profits in the UK were down by almost a third at £205m. The UK accounts for roughly a quarter of the £12.7bn of revenues generated by Compass worldwide.'[2]

Later, the company announced that it was phasing out the Scolarest brand. Instead, its school catering operation would fall under the wing of its US-owned subsidiary Chartwells.

Would any of this have happened if Oliver hadn't been prepared to challenge vested interests and political inactivity? Probably not. Oliver wasn't the first person to push for better standards in school meals – the Soil Association was already campaigning hard – but it was the power of TV that really changed hearts and minds. A government that had previously shown no interest in nutritional standards in schools coughed up an additional £280m. Businesses that had been doing very nicely selling highly processed foods to the family market had to raise their game.

In embracing controversy, in holding up the Twizzler as an emblem of all things bad, Oliver demonstrated that a bold controversial statement made in a very public arena can change the game. He would take that lesson forward to his next campaign.

MURDER MOST FOWL

'Hi guys, once again we're tackling a controversial subject', Oliver announced cheerfully ahead of the credits on *Jamie's Fowl Dinners*.

But while the cheeky 'mockney' persona was familiar, the campaigning chef hinted at something darker ahead. The programme was focused on chickens and eggs. The aim was to show the audience how birds were kept and slaughtered to feed the British appetite for poultry. And in showing the realities, he hoped to persuade the audience to think about the welfare of the animal and make choices accordingly.

'If we show you where the cheap meat comes from, next time you go shopping you'll make better choices', he said.

Statistics were chosen, of course, to make a point. Within minutes of the programme starting Oliver had revealed that 27 chickens are culled per second. Minutes later, he declared that pound for pound, chicken was cheaper to produce than dog food. 'That is insulting', he said.

And the programme darkened from there. Live and on screen Oliver supervised the gassing of male chicks, a practice necessary for the egg production industry simply because they won't grow to be productive birds. Seconds later, to gasps from the audience, he fed the dead birds to a grateful snake. Captive birds of prey and snakes, we were told, are the main beneficiaries of this industry's collateral damage.

As television goes, it was disturbing and captivating in more or less equal measure. Just as Oliver had blown the whistle on the contents of a Turkey Twizzler, he was now pulling back the veil on the poultry industry's dark secrets. How birds were reared, kept and slaughtered – it was all on screen.

In terms of impact, the opening minutes of the programme were very much in the tradition of the no-holds-barred, make-em-sit-up-and-take-notice PR stunt. Most of us had seen documentaries before, about the conditions under which chickens and hens are reared, but this was something new. The programme was presented in the format of a gala dinner. On hand were members of the public and representatives of the food industry. They would be asked to watch the live demonstrations and recorded film footage before tucking into a hearty meal of chicken. Those of us watching at home could be thankful we weren't there.

The programme was a companion piece to *Hugh's Chicken Run*, a series fronted by River Cottage chef Hugh Fearnley-Whittingstall in which he contrasted the conditions of intensively farmed birds with those of animals reared according to RSPCA standards. That too had its shock moments, notably when Fearnley-Whittingstall wept as he broke the necks of sick birds reared in wretched conditions.

Oliver publicly criticized Sainsbury's, a move that jeopardized his relationship with the firm.

While both shows had a profound impact on those who watched them, the long-term impact was harder to measure than, say, the outcome of *Jamie's School Dinners*. In the latter, once Oliver had the support of government, and key industry players had bought in, there was an opportunity to bring about rapid and real change in an area that was, after all, subject to the control of policy makers.

In contrast, *Jamie's Fowl Dinners* and *Hugh's Chicken Run* were setting out to change public opinion and habits of consumption rather than influence policy at either national or local government level.

The task was daunting. In principle, few people would argue that higher welfare standards are a good idea. But in practice it's difficult to wean people away from cheap, intensively reared meat or battery produced chickens. Low-income families in particular argue that the welfare of animals comes behind the priority of securing nutritious and affordable food for their tables.

Oliver and Fearnley-Whittingstall were also hoping to convince the supermarkets to switch and encourage consumers to buy ethically reared produce. That was also a difficult task. Representatives of all the major supermarkets were invited to the Fowl Dinners gala, but only the Co-op turned up. A clearly rattled Oliver publicly criticized Sainsbury's, a move that jeopardized his relationship with the firm.

But Oliver has continued to campaign and, in doing so, has helped change the mood music surrounding the debate. Free range eggs have been widely available for many years, but thanks to his programme – and the campaigning of others – chicken raised according to the RSPCA's freedom food standards is now more widely available. Recently, he has turned his attention to pork and the welfare of pigs. The campaigning goes on, and controversial TV is one of his greatest tools.

NEGATIVE CONTROVERSY

Oliver's willingness to tackle controversial subjects has made him one of the most talked-about television personalities in the UK and around the world. Equally, his campaigning zeal has ensured that he himself is a controversial figure. There's a thin line that separates the passionate campaigner and the irritating 'do gooder', and there are plenty of people who would argue that Oliver regularly crosses that line.

His detractors were given ammunition by *Jamie's Ministry of Food*. Setting aside animal welfare issues, this was a TV series that saw Oliver once again donning the mantle of ambassador for food. Travelling north, he stopped at the Yorkshire town of Rotherham where he set about the task of encouraging its citizens to eat better.

Some asked was this a series made by a well-intentioned young man with a real concern about diet, or was it the product of a TV production company owner looking for another juicy subject? Was there a genuine desire to help the people of Rotherham or was Oliver merely developing his own career on the back of a community blighted by higher-than-average unemployment and lower-than-average wages?

What we saw on the screen was certainly a clash of cultures. Oliver may have been an Essex boy born and bred but as the front man for a Channel 4 series he was the epitome of metropolitan life. With his high income, carefully tended hair and trendy clothes, he was in stark contrast to at least some of the people he met in the streets and kitchens of Rotherham. His was a world of fresh pasta and vanilla pods. Theirs was a world of kebabs and potato crisps.

There was plenty of evidence that Oliver's hosts didn't welcome his presence. When attending a local match, he was met with a chorus of 'You fat bastard' from the crowds. As *The Guardian*'s Alex Renton observed: 'This [show] teeters close to being the nastiest sort of human zoo TV. See the woman who eats 12 packets of crisps a day (and, it was implied, nothing else)! You can hear the southern fairies (Jamie's self-description) chorusing ...'.[3]

Renton, writing in the paper's TV blog, was ultimately won over by the show. Others weren't – but you have to ask if Oliver should worry. Ever since *Jamie's Kitchen*, he has been apparently happy to allow his production company to cover his activities, 'warts and all': his swearing, his arguments with Jools, the backbiting of dinner ladies, the tantrums of teenagers and the indifference of industry chiefs as he revamps the school diet. Even his spat with Sainsbury's was public knowledge.

It all makes for great drama especially when he wins over those who were initially reluctant to fall for his charms. At the height of the *Jamie's School Dinners* campaign, a Rotherham mother was filmed pushing food through the railings of a school playground to feed a child that was being 'tortured' by Oliver's healthy meals. A few years later, Oliver was back in Rotherham swapping cookery tips with her and, seemingly, getting on very well indeed.

And that's been the secret of Oliver's television success: controversy = drama = ratings. And of course, high ratings keep the visitors coming to the restaurants and buying the cookery books, DVDs, kitchenware and branded sauces. It's a positive feedback loop.

But it's not just Oliver's profile that prompts consumers to buy his products and eat in his restaurants – it is trust in him that matters most. As a TV cook, Oliver has continually hammered home his belief that cooking is all about using the best (and where possible the most nutritious) ingredients. As a campaigner, he has argued passionately we would all be healthier, more alert and better able to cope with the rigours of life if we paid more attention to the food we eat. He has become an ambassador not just for food but for high quality and nutritious food. What's more he has gone out on several limbs to argue that case.

Oliver not only talks about food – he sells it, along with a batch of related products. And would he sell us sub-standard ingredients? Of course not. Would we emerge from one of his restaurants feeling short-changed? Of course not. His brand is indelibly associated with quality

DOING THE BUSINESS

Oliver not only talks about food – he sells it, along with a whole batch of related products. And would he sell us sub-standard ingredients? Of course not. Would we emerge from one of his restaurants feeling short-changed? Of course not. His brand is indelibly associated with quality.

There are hazards here. Oliver can't afford to let his standards slip and he has occasionally had to fend off criticism on this front. In 2009 he was forced to issue a statement when the BBC's *Watchdog* pointed out that his Garlic and Olive Pasta Sauce had 5.3 grams of salt in half a jar. Oliver responded by saying that the consumers should use the highly flavoured sauce sparingly rather than simply pouring a whole jar into a pasta mix, but he admitted this wasn't clear on the label.

And he demonstrated a willingness to take action: 'The Olive, Garlic & Tomato pasta sauce we identified will be one of the first sauces on shelves with a reduced salt content and should be available in supermarkets this autumn.'

BE CONTROVERSIAL

Throughout his television career, Oliver has been a controversial and divisive figure and, on occasion, he has been prepared to push the boundaries of what is acceptable on the small screen. Yet despite more than his fair share of negative headlines, the controversial Oliver has remained a bankable property. This is how he has pushed the envelope while increasing his popularity.

- **Take on the big guys.** When he launched his campaign to improve school dinners, Oliver was taking on a whole raft of vested interests, including the government, local authorities and the food industry. His willingness to make a stand in the face of opposition won him many friends.

- **Stick to your guns.** Some of the most stubborn resistance to his school dinners campaign came from parents who resented being told how to feed their children. Going head-to-head with a swathe of the public is tricky ground for a TV presenter but Oliver never wavered from his central argument that children deserve to be fed healthy and nutritious meals.

- **Use shock tactics.** *Jamie's Fowl Dinners* – a TV show that set out to make its audience think about welfare issues before buying eggs and chicken – shocked its audience. While revelations about battery farming are nothing new, graphic depictions of how animals were kept and killed were unusual in a light entertainment format. By hitching his populist approach to a serious subject, Oliver made more impact than a dozen worthy documentaries. In the process he did no harm at all to his reputation.

- **Keep it real.** In addition to controversial subject matter, Oliver is himself a controversial presenter. Freed from the cheeky chappy persona of *The Naked Chef* series, he felt free to swear on television and engage in public displays of anger and frustration. He was also unafraid to show the strains in his marriage.

- **Stick at it.** It's easy to accuse TV presenters of taking a fly-by-night approach to the causes they espouse. After the cameras stopped rolling Oliver continued to make a stand on nutrition and animal welfare issues, thus retaining credibility with the public and other campaigners.

10
BE BOLD

'Everyone is advising me to slow down and pull in the reins, but I'm not listening to them. We're opening five restaurants this year. We've got people queuing up every night. You just have to get your pricing structure right. I don't think it all has to be doom and gloom.'[1]

That was Oliver talking to Nigel Farndale. With Britain in the midst of the deep recession, most businesses were battening down the hatches and putting expansion plans on hold. Oliver, in contrast, sounded more gung-ho than ever. Despite the credit crunch and the economic downturn he was stepping up his business activities and investing in new ventures rather than retreating to a country mansion to count cash already safely banked.

The plans he outlined were ambitious. Rather than leaving his hard-earned cash sitting in the bank, he would invest in a programme of restaurant roll-outs that would see the number of people on his payroll rise from 600 to more than 5000.

That last comment is typical of Oliver. Plans to expand his media and business activities are often couched in the language of social good. The mission of his companies is, after all, to encourage people to live better lives and eat better food, and he is rightly renowned for his social campaigning. But behind the altruism, there is clearly a huge amount of ambition and Oliver is prepared to take risks to get what he wants.

That should surprise no one. The willingness to take chances is an essential element in the make-up of the entrepreneur. From the one man band who gives up a regular salary to launch a consultancy to the private equity company investing millions in a high-tech start up, the principle is the same. Unless you're prepared to risk money or reputation or perhaps even your own health and welfare to follow through on a business venture, the opportunity will simply wither on the vine.

The importance of boldness or bravery can't be underestimated. Entrepreneurs tend to be more comfortable taking risks: they're prepared to put up their own money – and sometimes other people's cash – to pursue a dream or an idea to its logical conclusion. They'll put credibility on the line too. With every new idea or business venture there's a chance that it will fail. You don't fire the starting gun with the expectation that the whole project will come down in flames, but the possibility is always there.

In a rapidly changing marketplace, simply leaving money in the bank can be the riskiest strategy of all

The spectre of failure tends to be a deterrent and not just because of the cash. Failure itself can be a hard thing to live with and the natural inclination of many of us is to keep our heads safely below the parapet. If we don't strive, we don't suffer the stigma of failure. But then we don't succeed either. As the former chairman of Coca-Cola – Roberto Goizueta – once put it: 'If you take risks, you may still fail; but if you do not take risks, you will surely fail. The greatest risk of all is to do nothing.'

In other words, there's a strong correlation between a willingness to take risks and success. But there is, of course, another side to the coin. Risk taking and success are close bed fellows but so too are risking taking and failure. A decision to invest your life savings on a business venture could make you rich but it might also bankrupt you. Of course, you won't know either way until you've invested cash, energy and several years of your life testing your business idea in the market place.

The risk imperative doesn't begin and end with the establishment of a business and the initial investment. As a company grows, new opportunities present themselves. It could be a chance to break into an overseas market and reach millions of new consumers. It could be a major order from a supermarket chain. Or it could be a successful piece of research and development that has the potential to become a world-beating product. In all these scenarios, the chances are that a business will have to decide whether or not to invest money and management time up front, in the hope of reaping big rewards a few months or years down the line. In some cases, the managers will decide that the risks outweigh the potential benefits and sit tight.

Any business that is overly reliant on one or two major customers faces disaster if they look elsewhere or pool their contracts. As a TV presenter, Oliver owed his success to the BBC and when they didn't commission another one he was left high and dry

That could well be the right thing to do. Let's say a company is doing well selling an established range of products in a market it knows well. Developing and launching a new product – perhaps aimed at a different market – will not only cost money but also management time. In a worst case scenario, the failure of that new product could have a hugely damaging impact on the existing business as a whole. Diverting resources to a new venture can be disastrous if not managed, researched and funded properly.

On the other hand, markets change and consumers seek new things. In rapidly changing times, simply leaving money in the bank can be the riskiest strategy of all.

DON'T JUST STAND THERE, DO SOMETHING

In the early days of his television career, Jamie Oliver didn't come across as a particularly bold or entrepreneurial figure. Early success on the TV was due as much to the happy accident of being in the right place at the right time. At the time when he was 'discovered' working in the kitchens of the River Café Restaurant, Oliver was content to learn his trade and draw a decent salary. He certainly wasn't pro-actively sending his CV to the TV producers of Soho, or spending cash filming a show reel. Indeed, according to his biographers, he had some initial doubts about relinquishing shifts at River Café to pursue an uncertain television career.

Of course, once his face, vowel sounds and cookery skills made their first appearance on the television, success was assured. The first series of *The Naked Chef* was hugely popular in the UK and around the world, his cookery books were best-sellers and with more shows in the pipeline, he was on his way to becoming a very wealthy young man.

But he also relied on other people for his success. As a presenter, he was a talented figurehead but his destiny was in the hands of a broadcaster (the BBC), a production company (Optomen) and the viewing public. Without him there would have been no Naked Chef but there would have been a myriad of other cookery shows. Oliver needed the production machine, but it didn't necessarily need him. That point was brought home forcibly when the BBC decided not to commission *The Naked Chef* for a fourth series.

The Oliver of the late 1990s and early 2000s was a high-risk proposition. Any business that is overly reliant on one or two major customers faces disaster if they look elsewhere or pull their contracts. As a TV presenter, Oliver owed his success to the BBC and when they terminated his contract, he was left high and dry.

Well almost. In financial terms, he was still selling books and had established himself as the face of the Sainsbury's supermarket so, for the time being, he was financially secure. But the Oliver brand was built on the TV show. Too long away from the airwaves and he would be a less valuable commodity both as an author and a supermarket endorsee.

Perhaps Oliver's departure from the BBC roster of star presenters was a wake up call. Cast into the dead air that surrounds a presenter without a show, a much bolder Oliver began to emerge: someone who was prepared to take the risks necessary to expand and diversify his business.

ATTACK IS THE BEST FORM OF DEFENCE

The launch of the Fifteen restaurant and charitable training organization was a watershed in Oliver's career. In retrospect, we can see (as recounted in previous chapters) how the TV series associated with Fifteen refreshed and deepened his brand, making him a much more popular and bankable figure. That's with the 20/20 vision of hindsight. At the time, his decision to work with a bunch of unemployed teenagers was bold on a number of levels.

Firstly, he was putting his own money into the project. By 2004 he had invested £1.7m, with Fifteen draining funds from his own earnings. At one point he mortgaged one of his properties to get the Fifteen Foundation and the restaurant up and running.

Then there was the nature of the project itself. Until then, Oliver's TV work had taken place in a tightly controlled environment. His recipe shows may have been lively and occasionally controversial, they may have given the impression of being freeform and unscripted, but really he was working with professionals to produce an entertaining and informative programme in a specific format.

The risk that difficult teenagers would fail to come through was also ever-present, but again Oliver approached the Fifteen with a fine degree of caution and understanding of the task he was taking on

Jamie's Kitchen – the series that followed the progress of Fifteen – brought a new touch of anarchy to his shows – in the shape of the unemployed, potentially unreliable and unpredictable trainees who would (hopefully) learn the skills of cooking and staffing the restaurant.

The risks were evident on screen as the disparate bunch of trainees were cajoled and persuaded into shape. When the series started, there were no guarantees that Oliver and his team of expert chefs and trainers would succeed in producing fifteen people capable of working in the country's best kitchens.

Arguably the real risks were off-screen. *Jamie's Kitchen* wasn't just a reality show, it was the chronicler of a real life experiment. Once the cameras had gone, Oliver's own reputation would stand or fall on whether Fifteen could continue to pull in the customers, make money and recycle its profits into further training.

The risk was never more evident than when the 'great and good' of the restaurant world turned up to the opening night when Oliver and his team of trainees cooked for the industry. *The Times* described the scene in November 2002: 'Major chefs such as Antonio Carluccio, Fergus Henderson of St John and Mark Edwards of Nobu tucked napkins into their collars and waited, drooling, like cheetahs tracking a lame gnu. The doyenne of food critics, Fay Maschler, took a corner table.'[2]

And, of course, once the celeb writers, critics and restaurateurs had gone, Oliver – or to be more precise, the people he hired to run Fifteen – had to carry on repeating the trick night after night, year after year. Drawing exclusively on unemployed teenagers – some with real problems – he had to run a restaurant that could pull in punters and pay for itself. The project consumed money for some time and it gave its critics much to comment on. But today Fifteen is seen as a genuine success story and a flagship for entrepreneurship. In short, the bold move paid off.

CALCULATED NOT FOOLHARDY

The Fifteen project was a risk but it wasn't foolhardy. For starters, by selling the concept to Channel 4 as reality TV show, it had the immediate effect of returning Oliver to his natural home – the TV screen.

The financial risk was genuine but by the time *Jamie's Kitchen* hit the screens Oliver was a wealthy man. His books were still selling, he had a lucrative contract with Sainsbury's and he had properties that could be mortgaged. Yes, he was putting his own money into the project, but he wasn't betting the farm. Had the Fifteen project gone belly up, he would have taken a reputational hit, but his involvement wouldn't have bankrupted him.

Oliver also managed the risk around the teenage trainees themselves. He understood the task he was taking on. While he was undoubtedly the star of the show, his training efforts were underpinned by the backing of professional restaurateurs such as the River Café's Rose Gray and Ruth Rogers, and Oliver's mentor at Neal's Restaurant, Gennaro Contaldo. To help him select trainees from the thousands who applied, Oliver also brought in tutors from Westminster Kingsway College and Hammersmith Catering College.

And of course, he didn't fail. Applicants were vetted and selected, training took place and in the end Oliver reaped the rewards of a successful television series while also setting up a sustainable restaurant business.

HARD TIMES

Fast forward to the present day and we find that Oliver has once again revealed bold intentions – this time through an aggressive roll-out of new businesses at a time when other companies are laying off staff.

By 2009, with the economy stagnant – and possibly still contracting – Oliver had opened Jamie's Italian restaurants in Oxford, Bath, Kingston, Guildford, London (Canary Wharf) and Brighton and was actively advertising for managers to run planned establishments in Cambridge and Reading. Overseas, Jamie's Italian was set to open in Dubai and across Asia. His expansion plans didn't stop there. In parallel with the restaurants he was also growing his Recipease food store business and a party planning company specializing in cookery lessons coupled with retail sales in the home.

So was this madness? Well, recessions – even deep recessions – aren't universally bad news for all businesses. While many companies struggle, others continue to perform well and some reap considerable rewards as the economy turns down. In the retail sector, a store that offers good value gains from the new mood of austerity. Oliver's own paymaster Sainsbury's has bucked all expectations by raising its revenues at a time when money is tight.

Like holidays, cars, theatre tickets, CDs and books, a night out at a restaurant is a discretionary spend but consumers will reach for their wallets if the product represents good value

The strategy is simple: emphasize a strong value/quality proposition. People still need to buy food and a grocer that can help them continue to eat well without knocking a hole in the family budget is on to a winner. Similarly, while the recession claimed an early victim in the shape of the CD, DVD and game retailer Zavvi (formerly Virgin Megastores), HMV has strengthened its position on the high street. Although home entertainment products are a so-called discretionary spend, a CD or DVD doesn't cost that much – they are affordable luxuries. While consumers may cut back on big ticket items such as cars and holidays, music, movies and games are still on the shopping list. HMV has cashed in. Beyond the high street, there have been other winners and losers. Low-cost airlines have strengthened their position in the market while flagship carriers such as British Airways (working from a much higher cost base and charging premium prices) have felt real pain.

Which brings us back to Oliver's opening point about getting the price points right in his restaurants. Like theatre tickets, CDs and books, a night out at a restaurant is a discretionary spend and consumers will reach for their wallets if the product represents good value.

At Jamie's Italian, prices start at £5 for a pasta dish – affordability is very much part of the package. Customers will invariably spend more than a fiver a head of course, but the value proposition is clear. For a relatively small outlay, the consumer can sample some 'Jamie Oliver magic' at a price that won't involve taking out a second mortgage. So, when Oliver began to roll out the Jamie's Italian concept, he had the right value proposition for the recessionary times.

And if you get that right, a recession is not necessarily a bad time to roll out a business. Commercial property is cheaper, redundancies mean that talented employees are easier (and often cheaper) to come by and, as rival business fail, there is less competition.

The problem is cash. The recession that began in 2008 was a direct result of a catastrophe in the banking system. With banks in a state of near collapse, new and existing businesses found it next to impossible to borrow the cash needed to launch new projects and in many cases they were denied the working finance necessary to pay wages and rents. Many of the companies that collapsed in the wake of the world financial crisis did so because their banks had withdrawn support.

Opening restaurants is an expensive enterprise, but Oliver is fortunate in that he can draw on his own reserves. As his 2008 accounts show, £1.5m of his earnings were diverted via a loan into the Jamie's Italian enterprise.

Another way to buck a recessionary trend is to seek out new markets. Oliver's plans to open Jamie's Italian restaurants in Dubai and across Asia is further evidence of an increasingly bullish approach to expanding his business. But it's also a strategy that makes good commercial sense.

The appeal of the Oliver brand has long been international and he has a high profile in Asia. The continent hasn't escaped the global recession entirely unscathed but the economies of China, India and Singapore continued to grow in the aftermath of the global credit crunch, while those of Western nations have stalled or gone into free fall. In the longer term, Asian economies are expected to grow at a much faster rate than their Western counterparts.

In setting out his stall in Asia and Dubai, Oliver is tapping into new, rapidly growing markets where there is a clear demand for European-style restaurants. There are certainly risks, but as we've seen, he and his team have sought out a partner – Tranic Franchising – that will itself be raising finance to fund the project. The financial risks, should the project fail, are shared with others.

Oliver has been bold, but not reckless. By taking chances he has cemented his reputation and expanded his business empire.

BE BOLD

Over the years Oliver has become bolder, both as media player and businessman, even to the point of expanding rapidly in recession. But he's covered his back. This is how he did it:

- **Recognize when the time is right to take a chance.** Oliver's move to set up the Fifteen Foundation and its associated restaurant was undoubtedly a bold move, but it was also necessary. The BBC's decision not to commission a fourth series of *The Naked Chef* was a severe blow and he was unable to find another broadcaster to take him on in a similar format. Launching Fifteen and creating a reality show around it was a huge challenge but the decision to press ahead refreshed his career.
- **Invest but don't risk everything.** The risks associated with Fifteen were financial as well as reputational. He reputedly sank £1.7m of his own money into the project and it continued to eat into his fortune long after the television cameras had stopped rolling. However, he had financial resources in the form of property that could be mortgaged, income from book sales and his Sainsbury's advertising campaigns. Some of this could be diverted to Fifteen without any threat to his well-being. He also invested his own money into Fifteen restaurants but, even allowing for that, his overall business interests turned a healthy profit.
- **Understand the market.** The Jamie's Italian chain was launched in the midst of recession and yet, according to Oliver, customers were queuing for tables every night. He puts that down to getting the price points right while offering a quality dining experience.

- **Seek out new markets.** Expanding into overseas markets is undoubtedly bold, but it also makes good business sense. The rapid expansion of Asia's economies has created a wealthy middle class with an appetite for Western-style restaurants. Oliver is in a good position to cash in on that appetite.

HOW TO DO BUSINESS
THE JAMIE OLIVER WAY

You could argue that Jamie Oliver is an accidental entrepreneur. If he hadn't been 'discovered' on a BBC 2 documentary on the River Café Restaurant he might still be labouring in relative obscurity.

And yet when given the chance, Oliver picked up the ball and ran with it – first creating compelling television and later exploiting his own popularity to both highlight ethical issues he felt strongly about, and to launch an increasingly diverse collection of successful business ventures.

For those who would like to emulate his success, this is how he does business.

1 BE YOURSELF, BUT MORE SO

Jamie Oliver is a natural television performer. From straight ahead recipe shows through to the reality TV of *Jamie's Kitchen* and *Jamie's School Dinners* he is a compelling presence. His TV persona is built around a big personality and an ability to communicate clearly and passionately. Today that persona is the basis of a very bankable and carefully constructed brand.

- Get a lucky break.
- Get the formula right.
- Play to your strengths.
- Be consistent in your branding.
- Give substance to the brand.
- Stay visible to your audience.
- Leverage your brand values into new products.

2 EXTEND THE BRAND

Like many TV performers, Oliver added to his income by writing spin-off books and releasing DVDs. That in itself would have been enough to ensure his financial security. But as his television career developed he seized the opportunity to launch a range of business ventures on the back of his popularity.

- Take control of your affairs.
- Build the business around the values people associate with you.
- Stick to your core competencies.
- Partner with others who can extend the reach of your brand.
- Plan for a sustainable business future.
- Ride the lifestyle wave.

3 BUILD ON WHAT YOU'RE GOOD AT

Today the Oliver empire embraces a range of very different ventures, but for the most part he has stuck close to what he knows. The Oliver brand is about food and foodie lifestyle, and the products sold in his name conform to that pattern.

- Get proper training.
- Build on your competencies.
- Sell what you understand.
- Recognize the scope of your chosen business sector.
- Cross sell within your sector.
- Use multiple points of contact.
- Use new media.

4 REMEMBER THE SOCIAL DIMENSION

Oliver acquired wealth very quickly but rather than simply banking the cash he was quick to put something back. The first manifestation of this was the establishment of the restaurant concept – Fifteen – as a social enterprise dedicated to training unemployed teenagers. The publicity given to Fifteen through the *Jamie's Kitchen* TV series raised the profile of social ventures. Fifteen continues to expand and has helped hundreds of teenagers. It has also done Oliver's career and brand no harm at all.

- Be passionate.
- Build a good team.
- Build something sustainable.
- Plan for succession.
- Invest in the dream.

5 BECOME THE FACE OF A SUPERMARKET

Oliver has had a symbiotic relationship with Sainsbury's for a number of years. Oliver's ad campaigns have helped to deliver a rising market share to the supermarket even in the midst of recession. Meanwhile the enduring relationship has provided Oliver with a regular source of cash to fund his other activities. The relationship hasn't always run smoothly but it continues to serve both parties well.

- Negotiate the terms of the deal.
- Retain your own brand values.
- Keep your paymaster at arms length.
- Know when to be diplomatic.
- Keep it fresh.
- Know your value.

6 DEAL WITH ADVERSITY

Oliver has had to deal with his fair share of criticism and setbacks. He's done it with energy, imagination and a willingness to try out new ideas.

- Keep your name in front of the public even when the TV show is axed.
- Come up with good ideas to get back in the public eye.
- Reinvent a brand that appears to be wearing thin.
- Move your business forward and diversify.
- Take control of the production process.

7 GO INTERNATIONAL

Having enjoyed an international profile from the early days of *The Naked Chef* TV series, Oliver has gone on to exploit his global popularity as celebrity and businessman. Today, he is planning to roll out restaurants across Asia and make TV programmes specifically for the US market.

- Make a name for yourself in new markets.
- Put in the work to build and then sustain an international profile.
- Franchise your business.
- Work with international partners.
- Make programmes or products for specific markets.

8 PROTECT THE BRAND

The larger a company becomes, the harder it is to preserve the brand values of its founders. Oliver's business is growing fast but he continues to present a consistent brand face to the world.

- Choose good people.
- Choose effective partners.
- Stay in control.
- Have a mission for the business.

9 BE CONTROVERSIAL

Always a divisive character, Oliver has, where necessary, been prepared to embrace controversial causes with no guarantees that his views will prevail. It's a high-risk strategy that has nonetheless served to deepen and strengthen his grip on the public imagination.

- Take on the big vested interests.
- Stick to your guns.
- Use shock tactics to make a point.
- Keep your personality real.
- Continue campaigning even after the cameras have moved on.

10 BE BOLD

Even in a recession Oliver was launching new restaurants. Indeed he has always been unwilling to let money hang around in the bank when it could be funding and expanding exciting ventures.

- Recognize when the time is right to take a chance.
- Invest but don't 'bet the farm'.
- Understand the market.
- Seek out new markets.

LAST WORD:

TOWARDS A SUSTAINABLE FUTURE

Jamie Oliver can be a hard man to pin down. When we see him on TV or read an interview with him in the press, we are really looking at three distinct entities. First there is the man himself: brash, opinionated, passionate and occasionally vulnerable. Then there is Oliver the brand: a saleable face that adorns magazines, food labels, kitchenware, packaging and ads for the Sainsbury's supermarket group, and a name that appears above the doors of restaurants. And finally – somewhere in the shadows – there is Oliver the astute and sometimes opportunistic businessman.

Unlike, say, Richard Branson, Oliver doesn't talk much about his life as a successful businessman. His brand is built around food, lifestyle and a passionate belief that individuals can make the world better. We don't expect to hear him talking about balance sheets, margins and brand extension. You can leave that sort of stuff to Bill Gates or Warren Buffet. It isn't cool.

But increasingly Oliver is seen as a businessman first and foremost and TV presenter and author second. It's not hard to see why. Unlike other successful TV celebrity personalities such as Jonathan Ross or Stephen Fry, Oliver employs a significant number of people. By his own estimate, his various businesses have a headcount of around 100, but that figure is expanded significantly when you factor in the waiters and kitchen staff in his restaurants. Over the next few years he expects to have more than 5000 employees on his books.

That's a major responsibility. A 5000 headcount will include a significant number of people with mortgages, families and ambitions to do well in life. While they remain in his employ, they'll be looking to Oliver and his senior management to take the steps and make the decisions that will secure their future.

And perhaps the biggest challenge facing Oliver is the creation of a business empire that will sustain itself when the time comes for him and his family to hand over the reins to others. Given his energy levels, it doesn't seem likely that he'll retire at anytime in the immediate future but there will come a time when the Oliver face will disappear from our screens – TV celebrity usually has a shelf life.

So what happens to the business when Oliver tires of hectic shooting schedules or the ratings fall and the shows are cancelled? That's a question that Oliver is probably asking himself. In his company mission statement, he pledges to create a portfolio of businesses that will be sustainable in his absence. In his own terms, this means being 'less dependent on Jamie the person and more on Jamie the brand'.

The expansion of Oliver's empire supports that goal. Television programmes rely on Oliver's presence. They are a clear product of Oliver the man, while also being instrumental in creating the brand and living its values.

RESTAURANTS ARE DIFFERENT

No one turning up at Fifteen in London or at a Jamie's Italian in Bath or Guildford will expect to see the great man toiling in the kitchen. That task is left to kitchen professionals who work according to a set of brand and quality guidelines laid down by Oliver and his management team. So as his business empire grows through restaurant openings, new stores and product licensing, the Oliver brand takes over from Oliver the man as the main factor driving the expansion of the business and customers' experiences with it.

Can the brand ever be entirely independent of the man? In the case of Fresh One, the production company, the answer to that question is probably yes. Oliver's involvement undoubtedly makes it easier for Fresh One's managers to pitch a show at the BBC, ITV or Channel 4, but the company now has a huge amount of experience in making compelling television. There is, therefore, no reason why it shouldn't survive as an independent production company if its founder retired next year.

With the restaurants and shops this is a more open question. Without Oliver in the kitchen, they must establish a reputation in their own right. Currently, their appeal is driven, at least in part, by Oliver's TV popularity. It remains to be seen whether they can sustain that appeal if the man at their centre assumes a more low-key public persona.

To date, Oliver has made all the right moves. He prides himself on working with creative, ambitious people who can move his companies forward, and he's successfully launched ventures based around his brand rather than his personality.

The next few years should reveal the extent to which Oliver has created a truly sustainable, a truly 'pukka' group of companies.

NOTES

THE LIFE AND TIMES OF JAMIE OLIVER

1   Farndale, Nigel, 'Jamie Oliver: "I know we're in a recession, but we can still buy British"', *Daily Telegraph*, January 24, 2009
2   'Trevor Oliver on running a family-friendly pub', *The Guardian*, June 13, 2009

CHAPTER 1

1   Oliver talking about the early days of *The Naked Chef* on Jamie Oliver.com
2   As recounted in Smith, Gilly, *The Jamie Oliver Effect*, Andre Deutsch, 2008
3   Hattenstone, Simon, 'Never before has a boy wanted more', *The Guardian*, September 24, 2005
4   Hardy, Rebecca, '"I'm so busy I can't enjoy my family," says Jamie Oliver', *Mail on Sunday*, September 18, 2009
5   *ibid.*

CHAPTER 2

1   Smith, Gilly, *The Jamie Oliver Effect*, Andre Deutsch, 2008 and Hildred, Stafford and Ewbank, Tim, *Arise Sir Jamie Oliver*, John Blake Publishing Ltd, 2009
2   Author, 'Article name', *Broadcast* magazine, month date, 2009
3   Norman, Matthew, 'A most palatable marriage', *Daily Telegraph*, August 24, 2002
4   Brierley, Danny, 'Jamie Oliver is back with yet another venture', *London Evening Standard*, January 12, 2009

CHAPTER 3

1   Burn-Callander, Rebecca, 'Lawrence Dallaglio launches pasta sauce brand', *Real Business* magazine, September 28, 2009
2   Barrett, Phil, 'Designing Jme: Jamie Oliver's new lifestyle website', www.thinkflowinteractive.com, March 27, 2009

CHAPTER 4

1   www.bis.gov.uk
2   Kelly, Annie, 'The numbers game', *The Guardian*, March 4, 2009

CHAPTER 5

1   Poulter, Sean, 'The Fat Lady puts heat on Jamie over farmed salmon', *Daily Mail*, December 20, 2004
2   *Ibid.*
3   Kilgallen, Katie, 'Christmas ads: Let battle commence', *Retail Week*, December 6, 2007

4   Viner, Brian, 'Jamie Oliver: Essex's culinary icon', *The Independent*, October 6, 2001

5   *Ibid.*

6   Wallop, Harry, 'Sainsbury's turns its nose up at Jamie Oliver', *Daily Telegraph*, February 5, 2008

7   *Ibid.*

8   MacMillan, Gordon, 'Jamie Oliver and Sainsbury's', *Brand Republic*, January 11, 2008

9   Stacey, Caroline, 'Jamie Oliver: Naked ambition', *The Independent*, June 4, 2005

CHAPTER 6

1   Whitehead, Jennifer, 'Jamie Oliver signs for another year with Sainsbury's', *Brand Republic*, May 10, 2004

2   Clarke, Anna, 'BBC and Sainsbury's fall out over Jamie Oliver ads', *Brand Republic*, April 11, 2001

3   'Jamie Oliver: school series cost me £350,000', *The Guardian*, August 22, 2008

4   www.JamieOliver.co.uk

5   Moir, Jan, 'Interview: Jamie Oliver', www.areyoureadytoorder.co.uk, 2001

6   'C4 admits faking scene', www.bbc.co.uk/news, July 16, 2007

7   Dowell, Ben, 'Yentob in "Noddy" controversy', *The Guardian*, September 7, 2007

CHAPTER 7

1   Tryhorn, Chris, 'Jamie Oliver's companies almost double profit', *The Guardian*, August 5, 2009

2   Moir, Jan, 'Interview: Jamie Oliver', www.areyoureadytoorder.co.uk, 2001

CHAPTER 8

1   Oliver's primer on his organization http://jamieoliver.me.uk/ var/docs/jo_bb_about018.pdf
2   Hattenstone, Simon, 'Never before has a boy wanted more', *The Guardian*, September 24, 2005
3   Cooke, Rachel, 'Has Jamie's Ministry of Food worked in Rotherham?', *The Guardian*, November 16, 2008
4   Brown, Maggie, 'What's Jamie cooking now?', *The Guardian*, May 15, 2006
5   Bennett, Alison, 'Patak's Page to grow Jamie Oliver venture', *The Grocer*, March 17, 2007
6   Oliver's primer on his organization http://jamieoliver.me.uk/ var/docs/jo_bb_about018.pdf
7   'Jamie Oliver's latest dining concept set for Asian expansion', *Tranic* press release, August 31, 2009
8   Oliver's primer on his organization http://jamieoliver.me.uk/ var/docs/jo_bb_about018.pdf
9   *Ibid.*

CHAPTER 9

1   'Turkey Twizzlers in school ban', BBC *Newsround*, March 7, 2005
2   Davoudi, Salamander, 'Compass sells SSP for 1.8bn', *Financial Times*, April 9, 2006
3   Renton, Alex, 'Jamie Oliver's Ministry of Food goes to Rother-ham', *The Guardian* Word of Mouth blog, October 1, 2008

CHAPTER 10

1   Farndale, Nigel, 'Jamie Oliver: "I know we're in a recession, but we can still buy British"', *Daily Telegraph*, January 24, 2009
2   Coren, Giles, 'A 15-gun salute for brave Oliver and his young army', *The Times*, November 15, 2002

INDEX

TREVOR CLAWSON

Trevor Clawson is a freelance business journalist specializing in fast growth companies, management , new media, technology and marketing. His work has appeared in the *Guardian*, the *Independent*, the *Sunday Times*, the *Mail on Sunday*, *Director* magazine, *Growing Business* magazine and *Revolution*. Prior to going freelance he edited a business teletext news service for BBC World television and two magazines - *e.Business* and *PLC Director*.